ELTON JOHN
GREATEST HITS
1970-2002

ISBN 978-1-4234-4570-8

HAL•LEONARD®
CORPORATION
7777 W. BLUEMOUND RD. P.O. BOX 13819 MILWAUKEE, WI 53213

Visit Hal Leonard Online at
www.halleonard.com

CONTENTS

STRUM AND PICK PATTERNS

This chart contains the suggested strum and pick patterns that are referred to by number at the beginning
of each song in this book. The symbols ⊓ and ∨ in the strum patterns refer to down and up strokes, respectively.
The letters in the pick patterns indicate which right-hand fingers plays which strings.

p = thumb
i = index finger
m = middle finger
a = ring finger

For example; Pick Pattern 2
is played: thumb - index - middle - ring

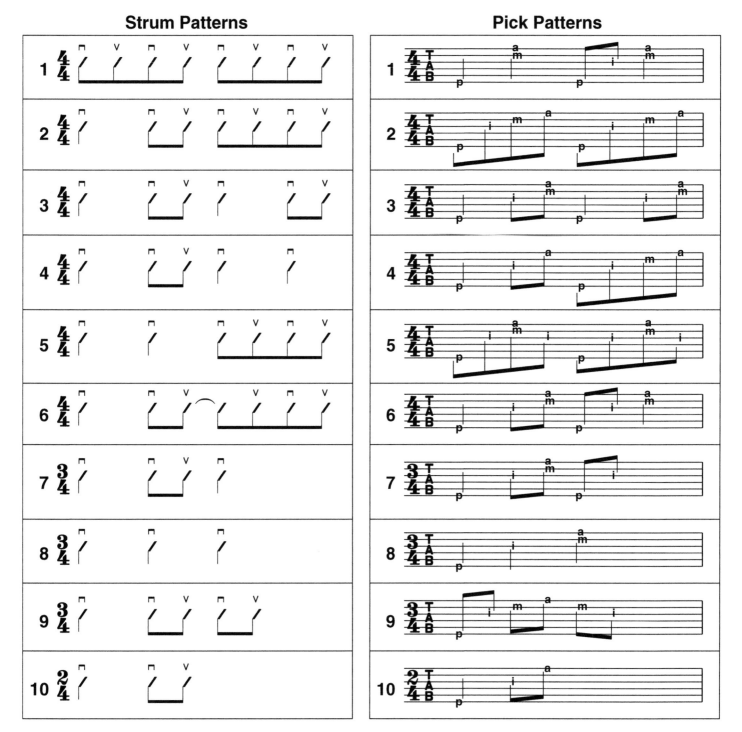

You can use the 3/4 Strum or Pick Patterns in songs written in compound meter (6/8, 9/8, 12/8, etc.).
For example, you can accompany a song in 6/8 by playing the 3/4 pattern twice in each measure.
The 4/4 Strum and Pick Patterns can be used for songs written in cut time (¢) by doubling the note
time values in the patterns. Each pattern would therefore last two measures in cut time.

Your Song

Words and Music by Elton John and Bernie Taupin

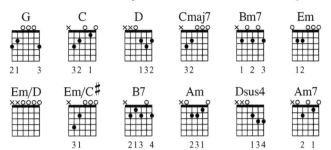

Strum Pattern: 2, 3
Pick Pattern: 3, 4

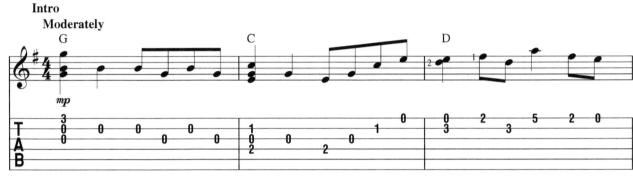

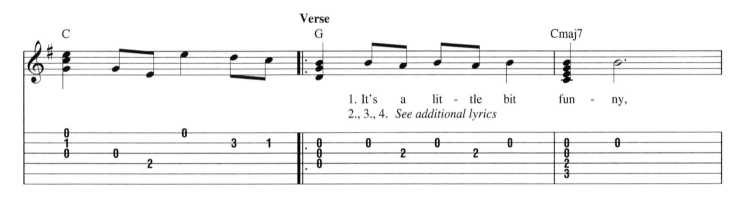

1. It's a lit - tle bit fun - ny,
2., 3., 4. *See additional lyrics*

this feel - ing in - side. _____ I'm not one of

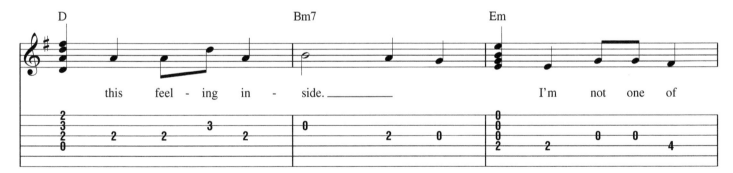

those who can eas - i - ly hide. _____

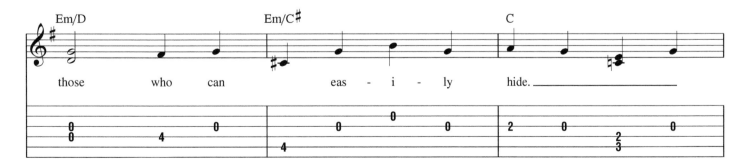

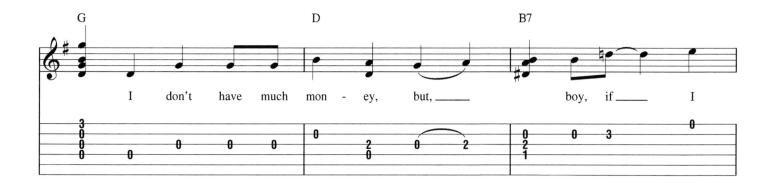

I don't have much mon - ey, but, _____ boy, if _____ I

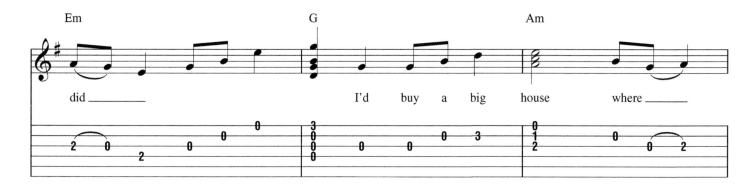

did _____ I'd buy a big house where _____

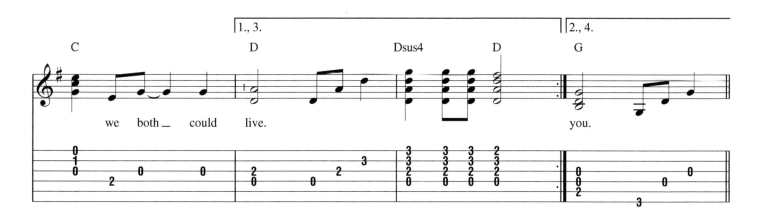

we both _ could live. you.

Chorus

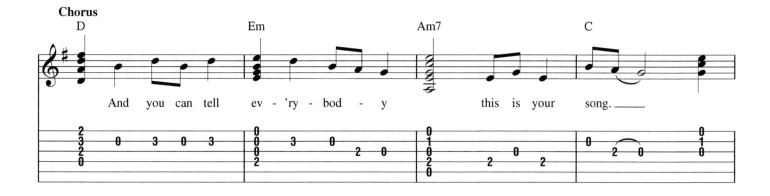

And you can tell ev - 'ry - bod - y this is your song. _____

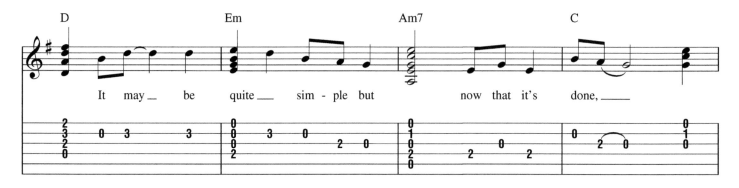

It may _ be quite _ sim - ple but now that it's done, _____

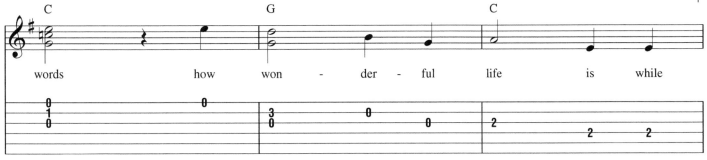

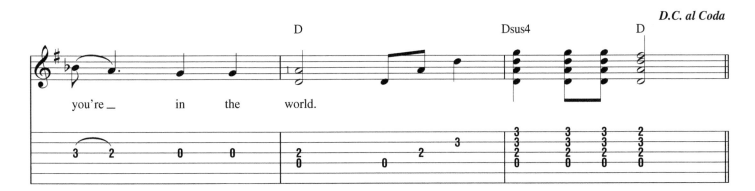

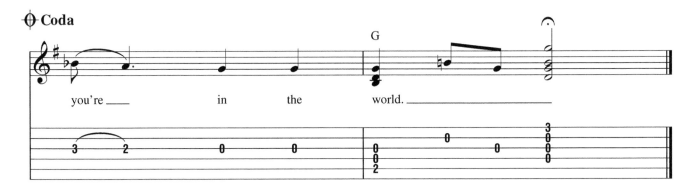

Additional Lyrics

2. If I was a sculptor, but then again no,
   Or a man who makes potions in a travelin' show.
   I know it's not much, but it's the best I can do.
   My gift is my song and this one's for you.

3. I sat on the roof and kicked off the moss.
   Well, a few of the verses, well, they've got me quite cross.
   But the sun's been quite kind while I wrote this song.
   It's for people like you that keep it turned on.

4. So excuse me forgetting, but these days I do.
   You see, I've forgotten if they're green or they're blue.
   Anyway, the thing is, what I really mean,
   Yours are the sweetest eyes I've ever seen.

Levon

Words and Music by Elton John and Bernie Taupin

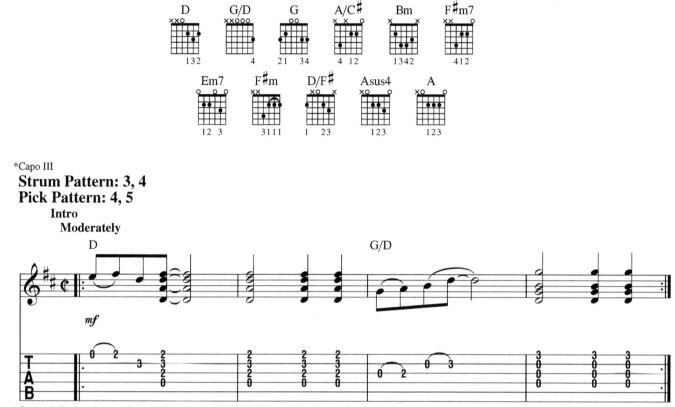

*Capo III

Strum Pattern: 3, 4
Pick Pattern: 4, 5

Intro
Moderately

*Optional: To match recording, place capo at 3rd fret.

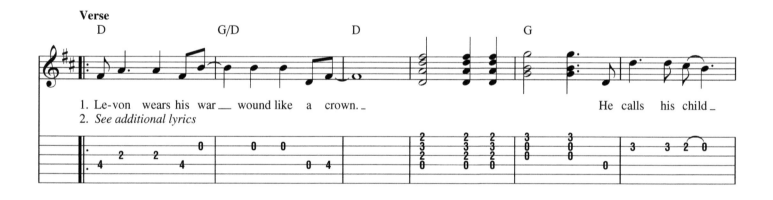

Verse

1. Le-von wears his war wound like a crown. He calls his child
2. *See additional lyrics*

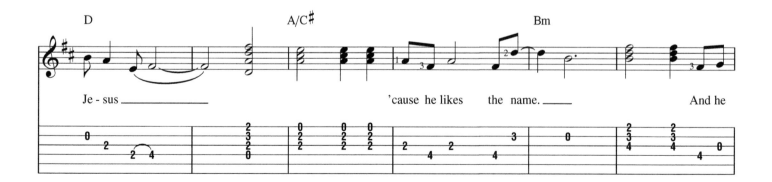

Je-sus 'cause he likes the name. And he

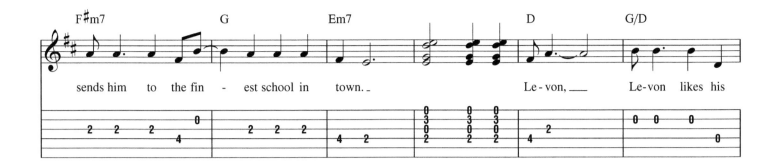

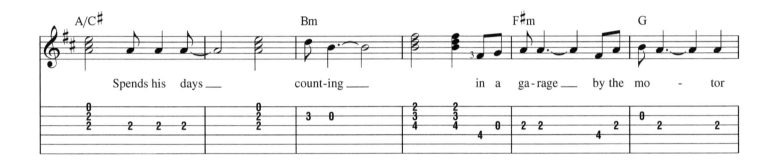

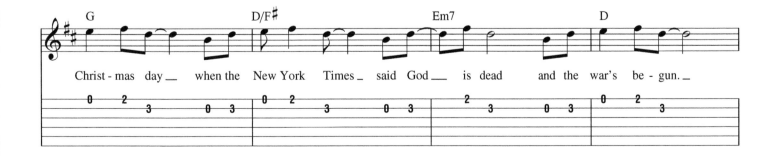

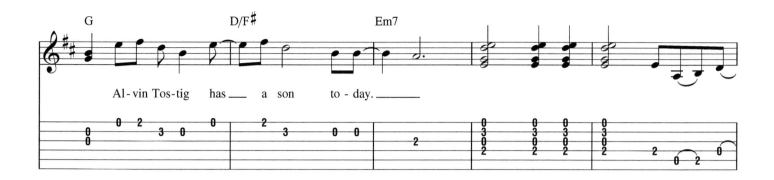

Al - vin Tos - tig has a son to - day.

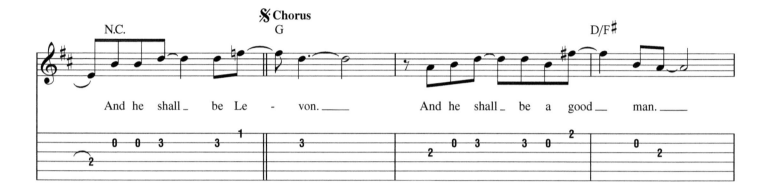

Chorus

And he shall be Le - von. And he shall be a good man.

And he shall be Le - von in tra - di - tion with the

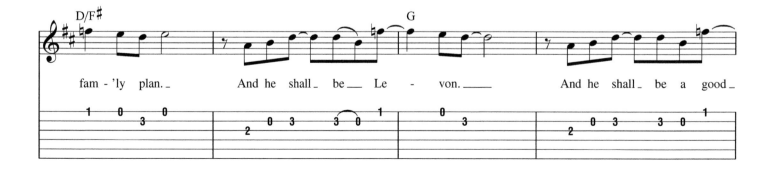

fam - 'ly plan. And he shall be Le - von. And he shall be a good

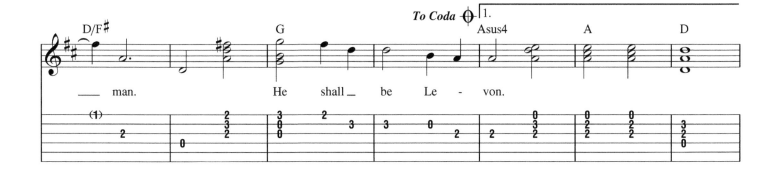

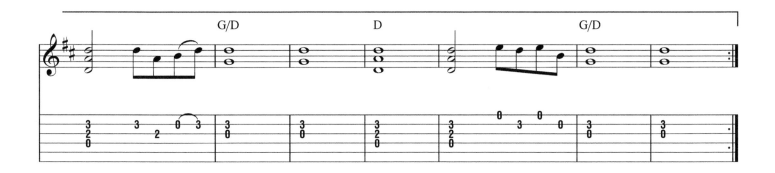

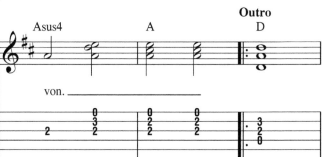

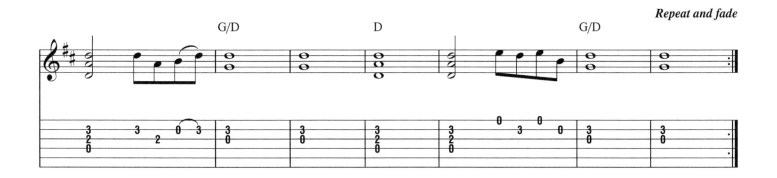

Additional Lyrics

2. Levon sells cartoon balloons in town.
His family business thrives.
Jesus blows up balloons all day,
Sits on the porch swing watching them fly.
And Jesus, he wants to go to Venus,
Leave Levon far behind,
Take a balloon and go sailing,
While Levon, Levon slowly dies.

Tiny Dancer

Words and Music by Elton John and Bernie Taupin

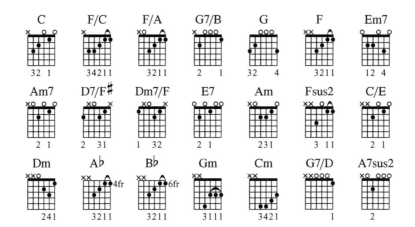

Strum Pattern: 3, 4
Pick Pattern: 4, 5

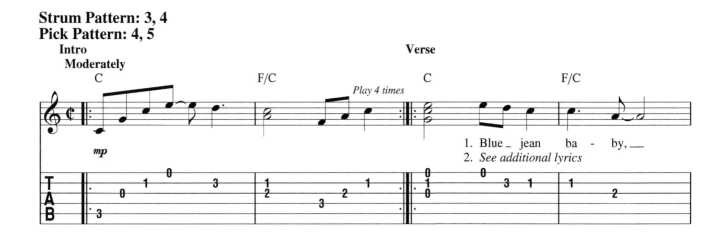

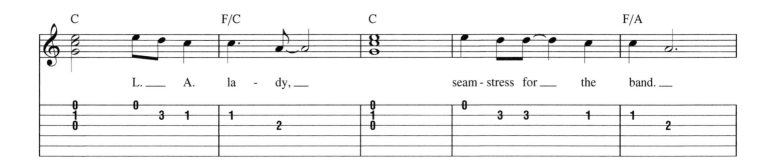

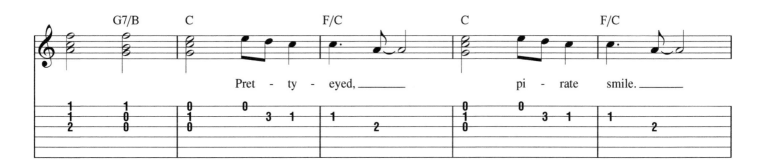

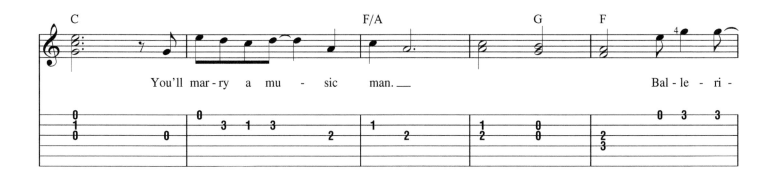

You'll mar-ry a mu - sic man. ___ Bal - le - ri -

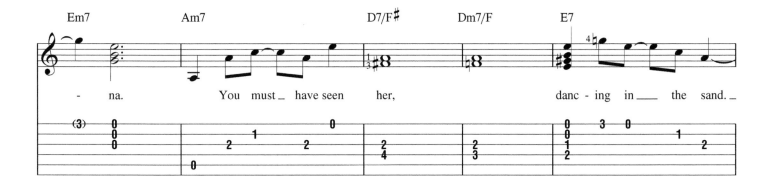

- na. You must ___ have seen her, danc - ing in ___ the sand. ___

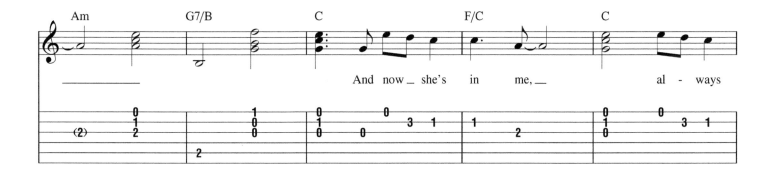

___ And now ___ she's in me, ___ al - ways

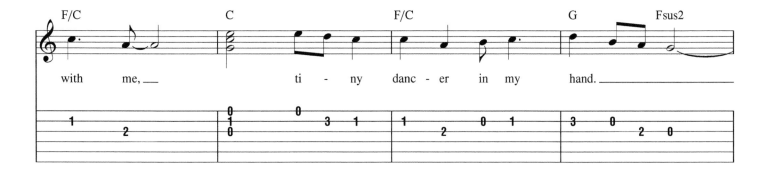

with me, ___ ti - ny danc - er in my hand. _____

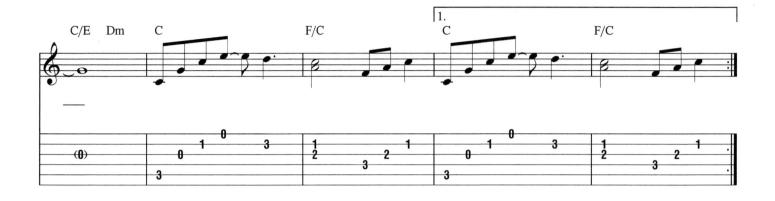

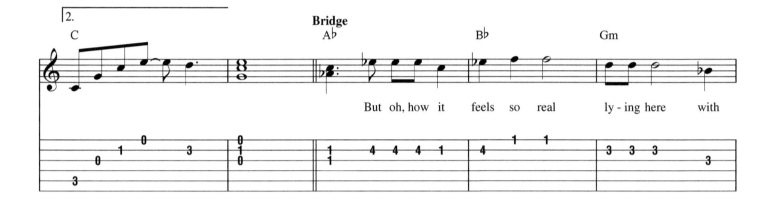

But oh, how it feels so real ly - ing here with

no one near. On - ly you, and you can hear me when I say

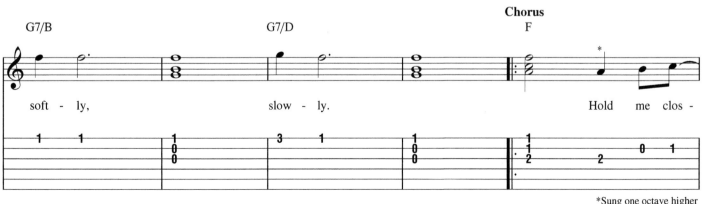

soft - ly, slow - ly. Hold me clos -

*Sung one octave higher throughout Chorus.

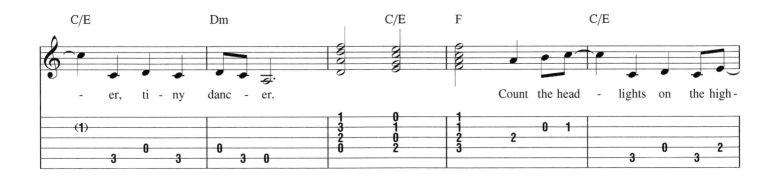

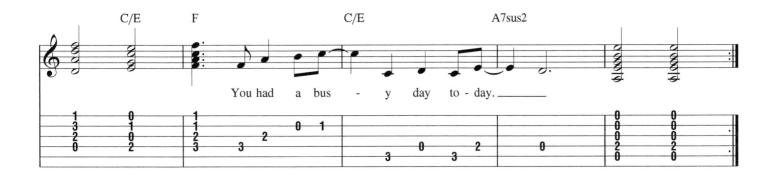

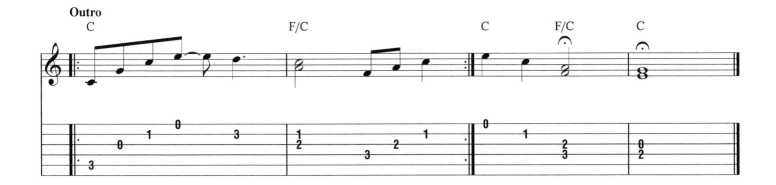

Additional Lyrics

2. Jesus freaks, out in the street, handing tickets out for God.
Turning back, she just laughs. The boulevard is not that bad.
Piano man, he makes his stand in the auditorium.
Looking on, she sings the songs. The words she knows, the tune she hums.

Rocket Man
(I Think It's Gonna Be a Long Long Time)

Words and Music by Elton John and Bernie Taupin

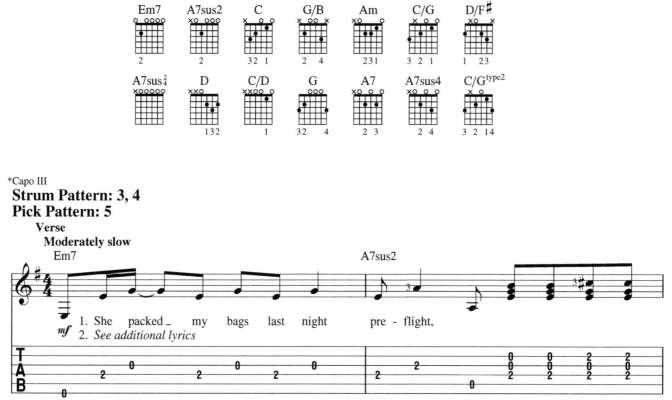

*Capo III

Strum Pattern: 3, 4
Pick Pattern: 5

Verse
Moderately slow

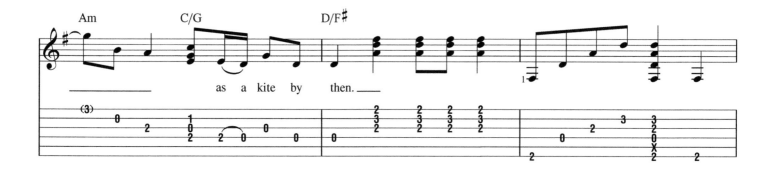

1. She packed my bags last night pre-flight,
2. *See additional lyrics*

*Optional: To match recording, place capo at 3rd fret.

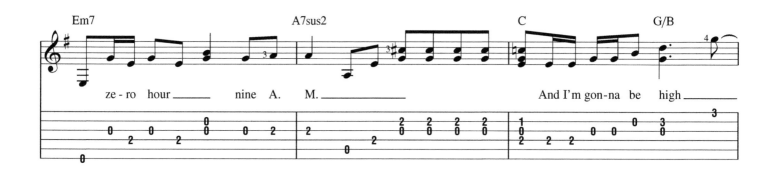

ze-ro hour _____ nine A. M. _____ And I'm gon-na be high _____

_____ as a kite by then. _____

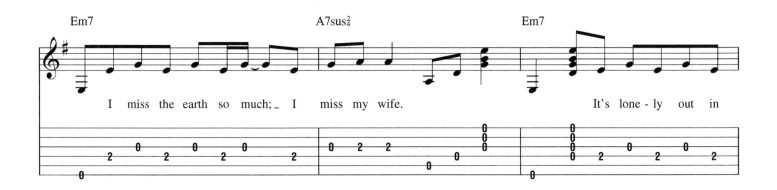

I miss the earth so much; _ I miss my wife. It's lone - ly out in

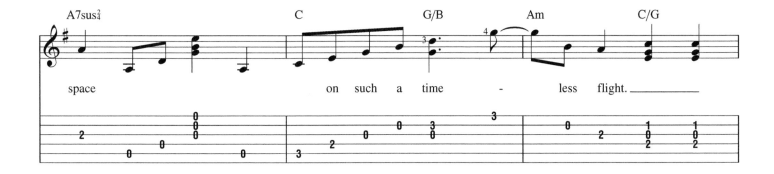

space on such a time - less flight. _____

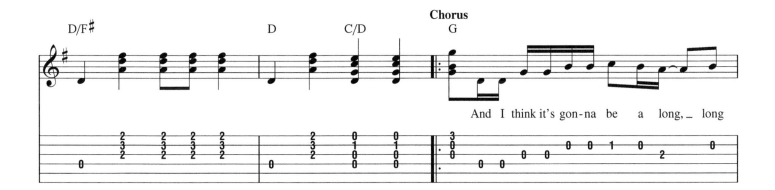

Chorus

And I think it's gon-na be a long, _ long

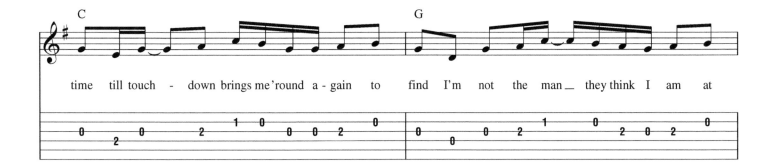

time till touch - down brings me 'round a - gain to find I'm not the man _ they think I am at

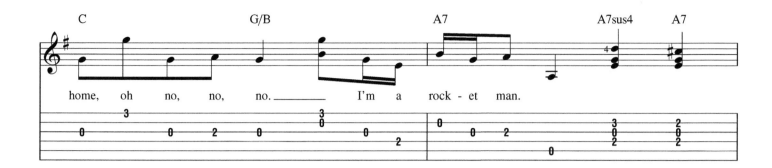

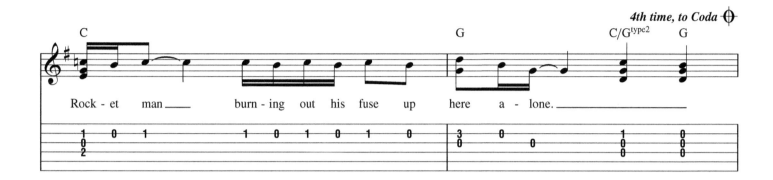

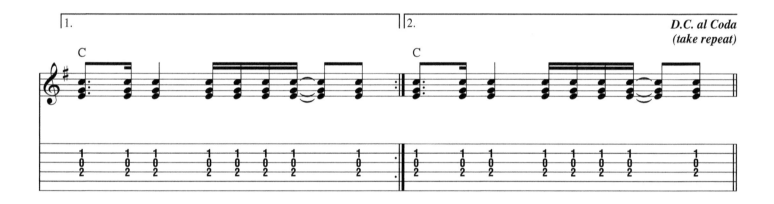

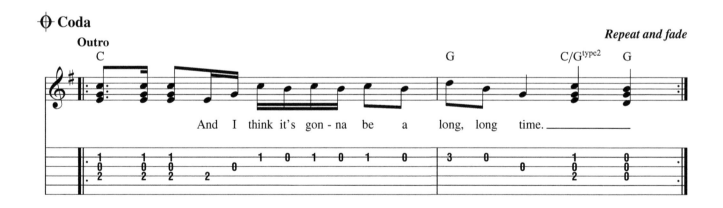

Additional Lyrics

2. Mars ain't the kind of place to raise your kids,
   In fact, it's cold as hell.
   And there's no one there to raise them if you did.
   And all this science I don't understand.
   It's just my job five days a week.
   A rocket man, a rocket man.

Crocodile Rock

Words and Music by Elton John and Bernie Taupin

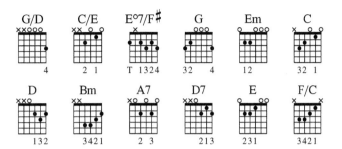

Strum Pattern: 3, 6
Pick Pattern: 4, 5

Intro
Moderately fast

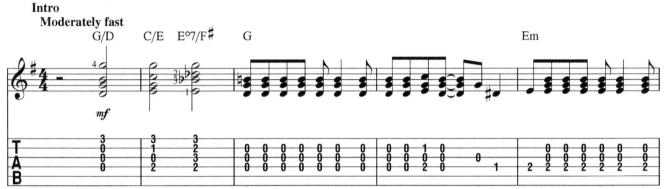

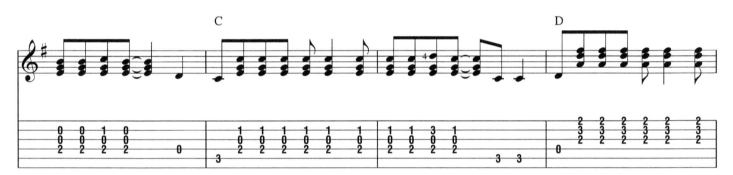

Verse

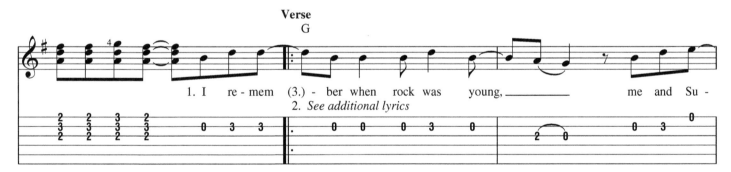

1. I re-mem (3.) - ber when rock was young, _____ me and Su-
2. *See additional lyrics*

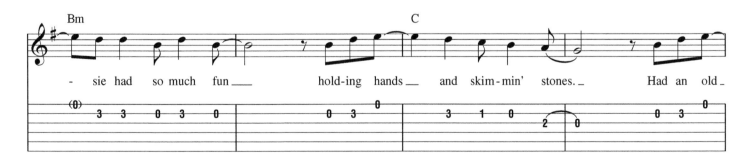

- sie had so much fun _____ hold-ing hands _____ and skim-min' stones. _ Had an old _

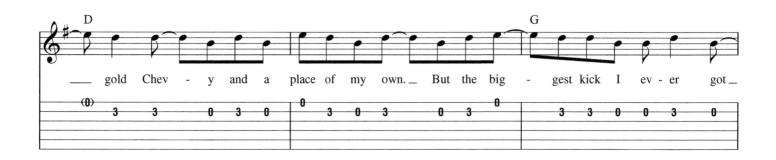

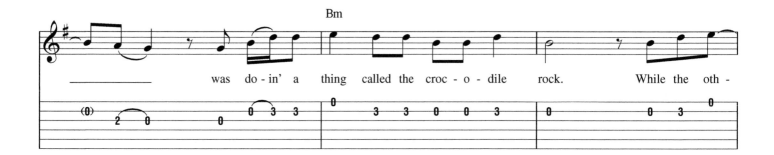

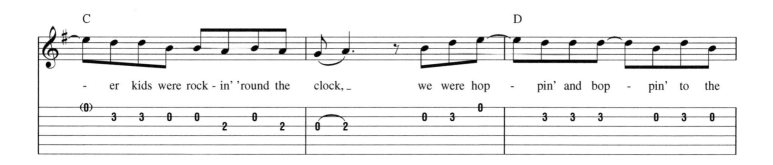

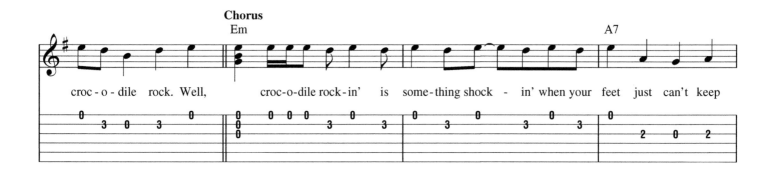

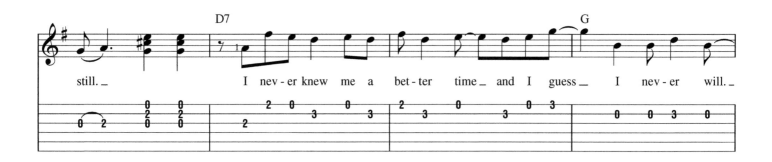

Oh, Lord - y, ma - ma, those Fri - day nights _ when Su - sie wore _ her

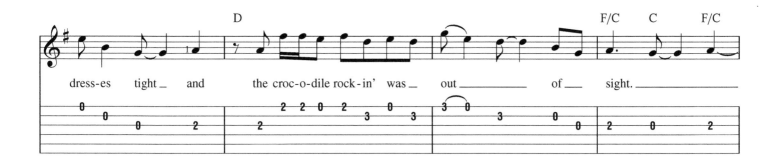

dress-es tight _ and the croc-o-dile rock-in' was _ out _____ of ___ sight. _____

Interlude

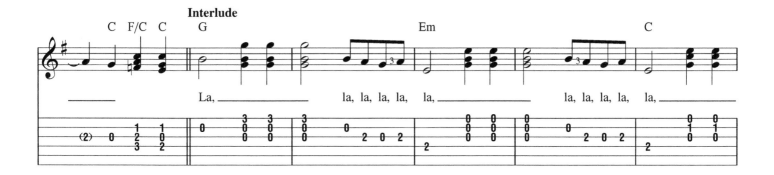

La, _____ la, la, la, la, la, _____ la, la, la, la, la,

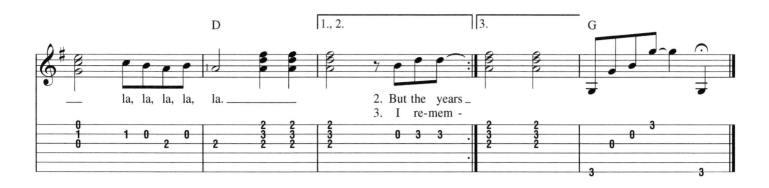

la, la, la, la, la. _____
2. But the years _
3. I re-mem -

Additional Lyrics

2. But the years went by and rock just died.
   Susie went and left us for some foreign guy.
   Long nights cryin' by the record machine,
   Dreamin' of my Chevy and my old blue jeans.
   But they'll never kill the thrills we got
   Burnin' up to the crocodile rock.
   Learning fast as the weeks went past,
   We really thought the crocodile rock would last.

Honky Cat

Words and Music by Elton John and Bernie Taupin

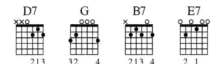

Strum Pattern: 6
Pick Pattern: 1, 4

Intro
Moderately fast

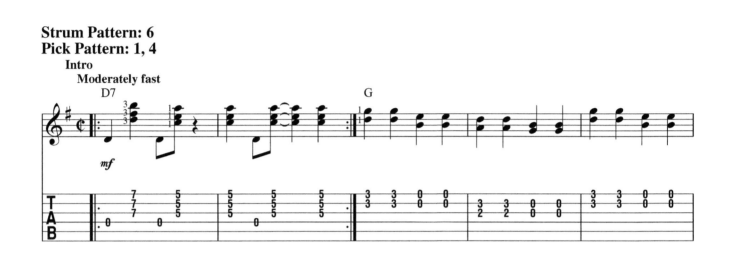

Verse

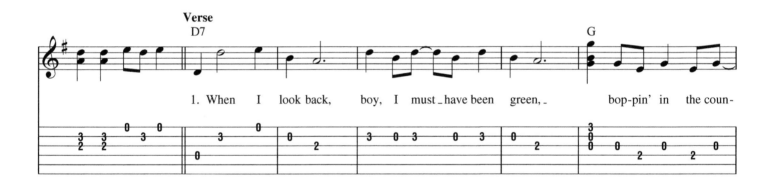

1. When I look back, boy, I must have been green, bop-pin' in the coun-

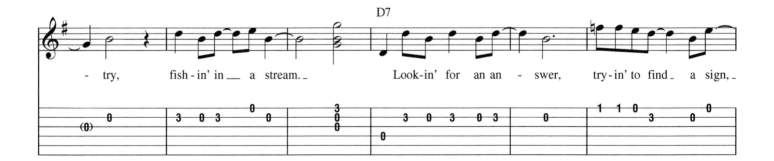

-try, fish-in' in a stream. Look-in' for an an-swer, try-in' to find a sign,

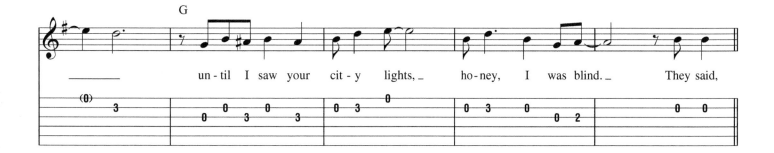

_____ un-til I saw your cit-y lights, _ ho-ney, I was blind. _ They said,

𝄋 Chorus

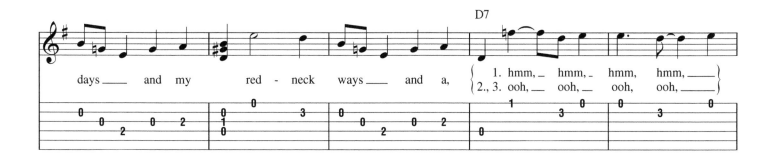

{1., 2. "Get}
{3. get} back, hon-ky cat, bet-ter get back to the woods." _ Well, I quit those

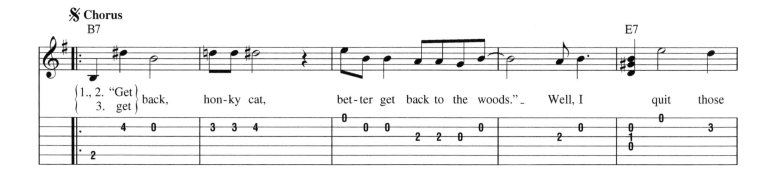

days _____ and my red-neck ways _____ and a, {1. hmm, _ hmm, _ hmm, hmm, _____}
{2., 3. ooh, _ ooh, _ ooh, ooh, _____}

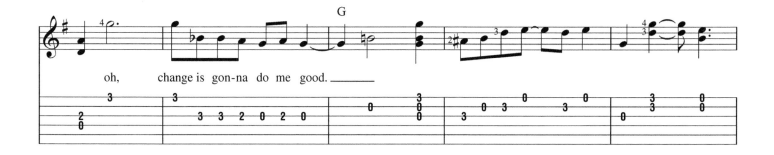

oh, change is gon-na do me good. _____

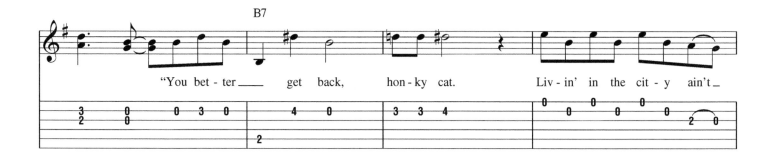

"You bet-ter _____ get back, hon-ky cat. Liv-in' in the cit-y ain't _

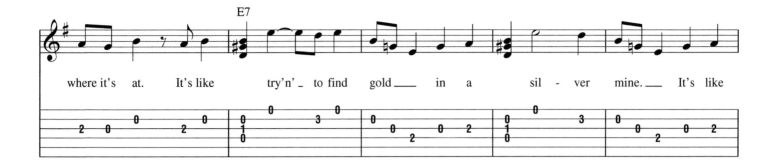

where it's at.	It's like	try'n'___ to find	gold___	in a	sil - ver mine.___	It's like

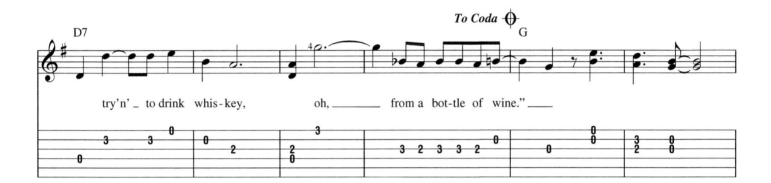

try'n'___ to drink whis-key,	oh, _____ from a bot-tle of wine." ____

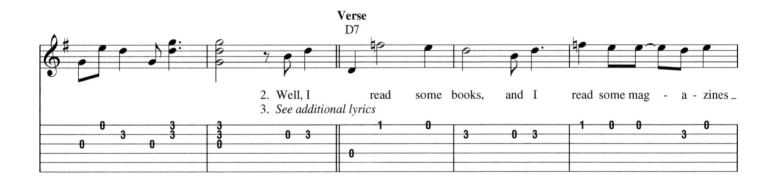

Verse

2. Well, I	read	some books,	and I	read some mag	- a - zines
3. *See additional lyrics*

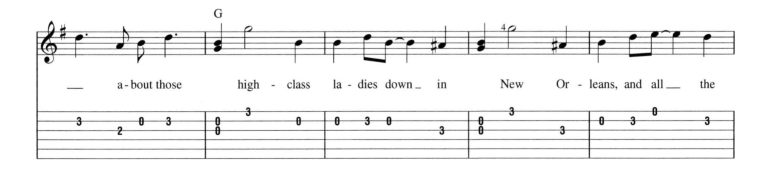

___	a - bout those	high - class	la - dies down___ in	New	Or - leans, and all___	the

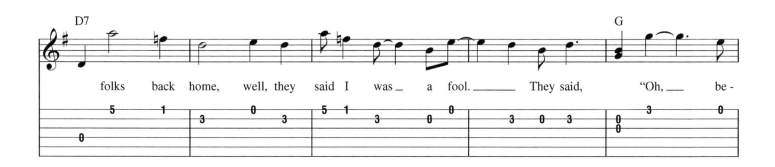

folks back home, well, they said I was __ a fool. _____ They said, "Oh, ___ be -

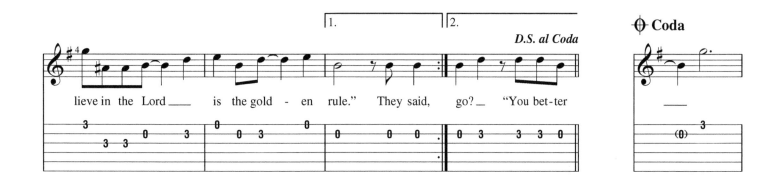

lieve in the Lord ___ is the gold - en rule." They said, go? __ "You bet -ter

Get back, hon - ky cat, get back hon - ky cat,

get back, ooh.

Additional Lyrics

3. They said, "Stay at home, boy, you gotta tend to the farm.
   Livin' in the city, boy, is, is gonna break your heart."
   But how can you stay when your heart says no? Ah, ah.
   How can you stop when your feet say go?

Daniel

Words and Music by Elton John and Bernie Taupin

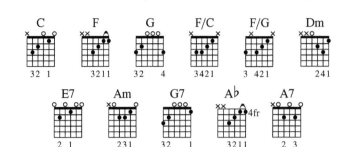

Strum Pattern: 6
Pick Pattern: 5

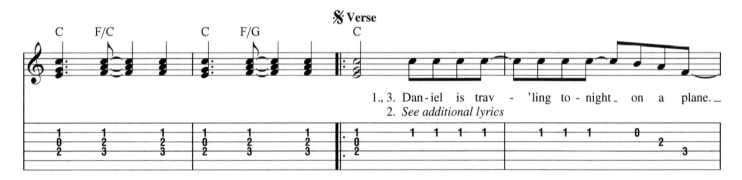

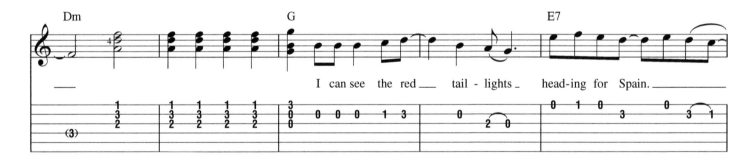

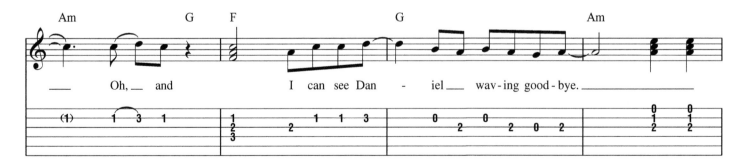

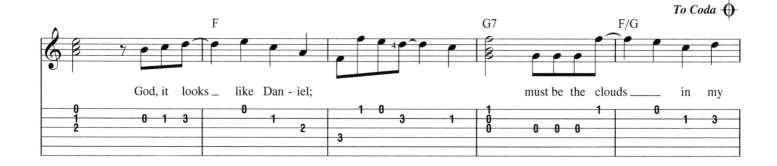

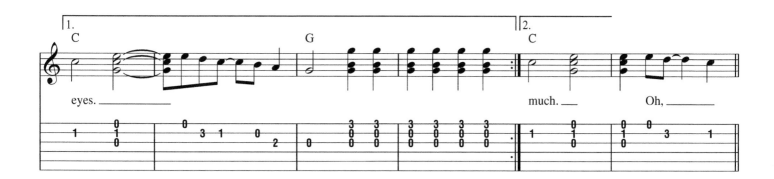

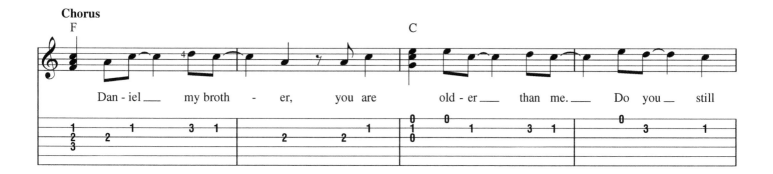

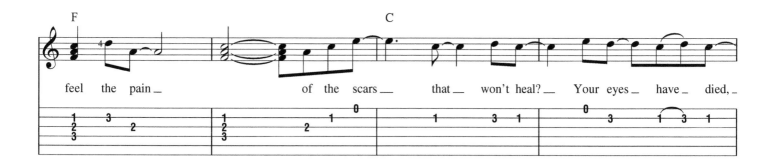

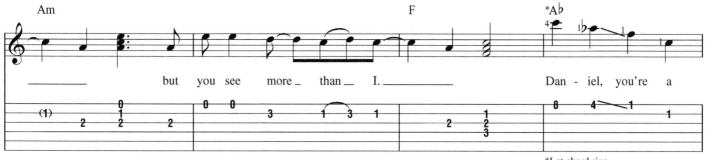

*Let chord ring.

27

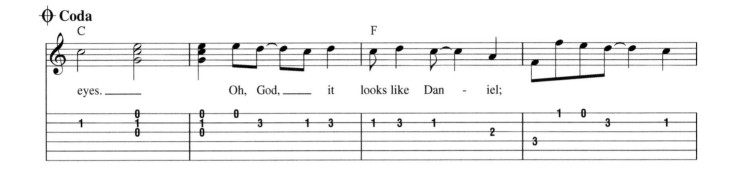

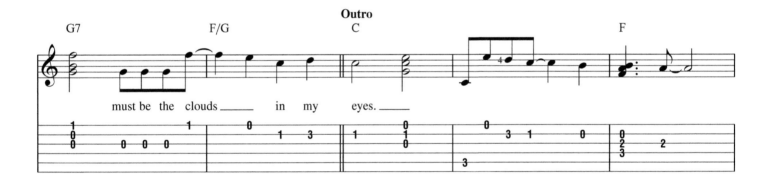

Additional Lyrics

2. They say Spain is pretty though I've never been.
Well, Daniel says it's the best place he's ever seen.
Oh, and he should know; he's been there enough.
Lord, I miss Daniel; oh, I miss him so much.

Saturday Night's Alright (For Fighting)

Words and Music by Elton John and Bernie Taupin

D   C   G   Am7   F   Bb

*Capo VII

Strum Pattern: 2, 3
Pick Pattern: 3, 4

Verse
Moderate Rock

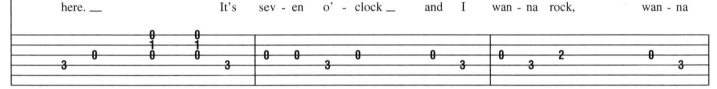

1. It's get-ting late, have you seen my mates; — Ma, tell me when the boys get

2. *See additional lyrics*

*Optional: To match recording, place capo at 7th fret.

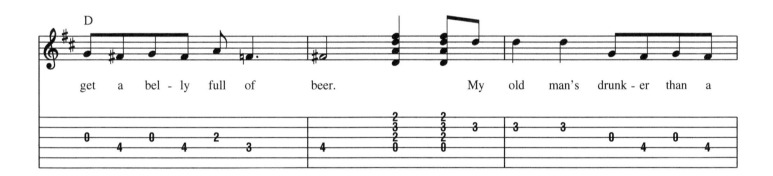

here. — It's sev-en o'-clock — and I wan-na rock, wan-na

get a bel-ly full of beer. My old man's drunk-er than a

bar-rel full of mon-keys and my old la-dy, she don't care. My

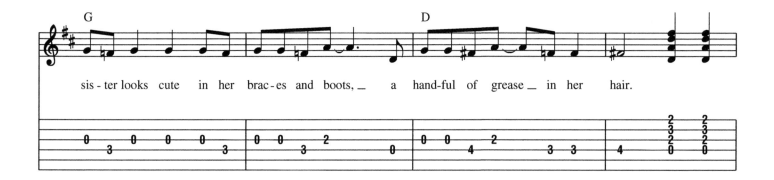

sis-ter looks cute in her brac-es and boots, _ a hand-ful of grease _ in her hair.

Chorus

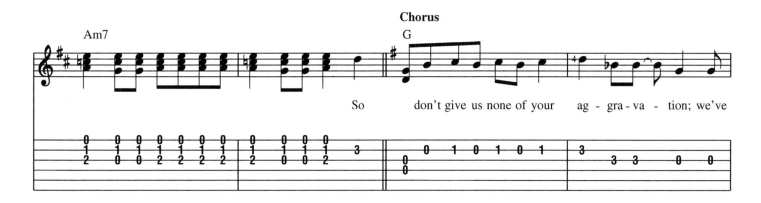

So don't give us none of your ag-gra-va-tion; we've

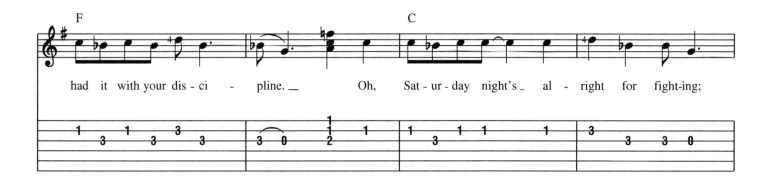

had it with your dis-ci - pline. _ Oh, Sat-ur-day night's _ al - right for fight-ing;

get a lit-tle ac-tion in. Get a-bout as oiled _ as a die-sel train, _

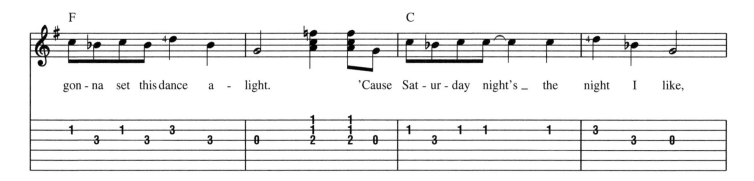

gon-na set this dance a - light. 'Cause Sat-ur-day night's _ the night I like,

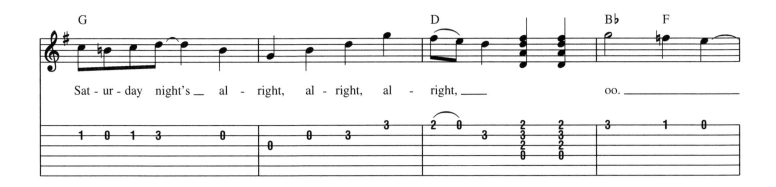

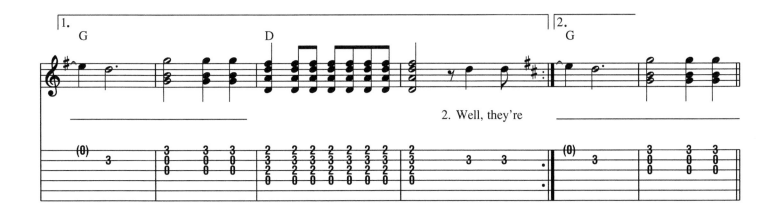

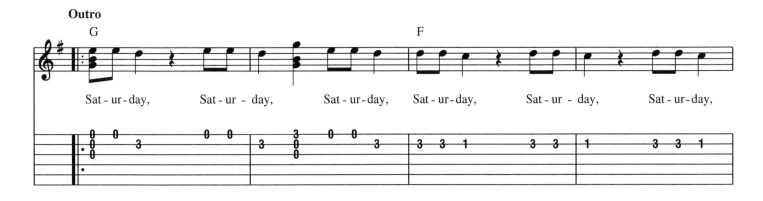

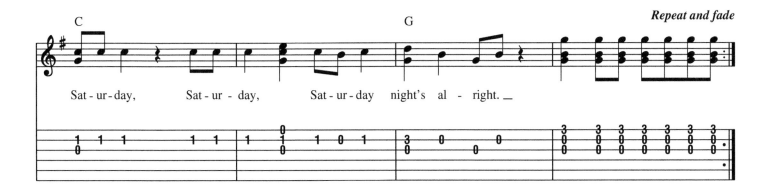

Additional Lyrics

2. Well, they're packed pretty tight in here tonight;
   I'm looking for a dolly to see me right.
   I may use a little muscle to get what I need,
   I may sink a little drink and shout out, "She's with me!"
   A couple of sounds that I really like
   Are the sounds of a switchblade and a motorbike.
   I'm a juvenile product of the working class
   Whose best friend floats in the bottom of a glass.

Goodbye Yellow Brick Road

Words and Music by Elton John and Bernie Taupin

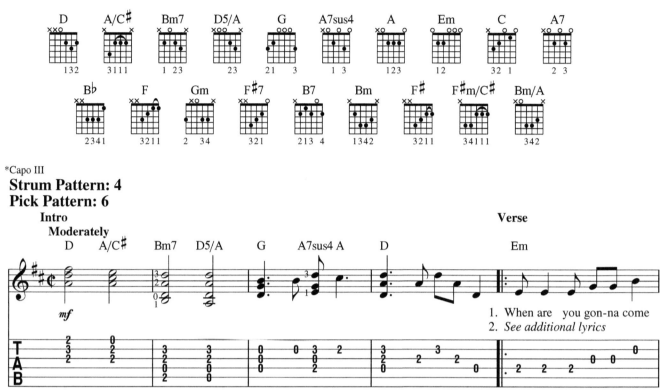

*Capo III

Strum Pattern: 4
Pick Pattern: 6

Intro
Moderately

1. When are you gon-na come down? ___ When are you go-ing to land? ___ I should have stayed ___ on the farm, ___ should have lis-tened to my ___ old man. ___ You know you can't hold ___ me for - ev - er. I
2. See additional lyrics

*Optional: To match recording, place capo at 3rd fret.

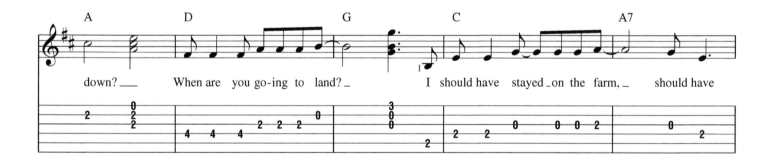

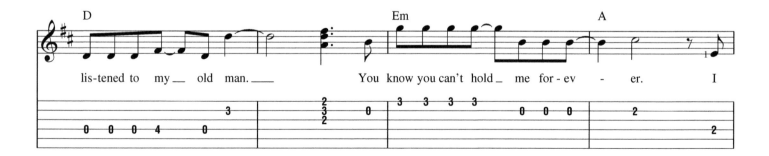

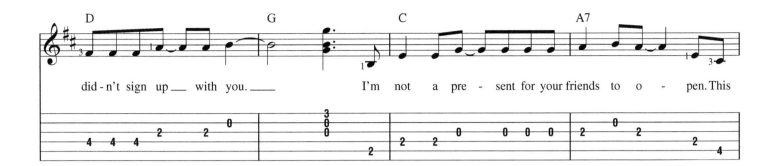

did-n't sign up ___ with you. ___   I'm not a pre - sent for your friends to o - pen. This

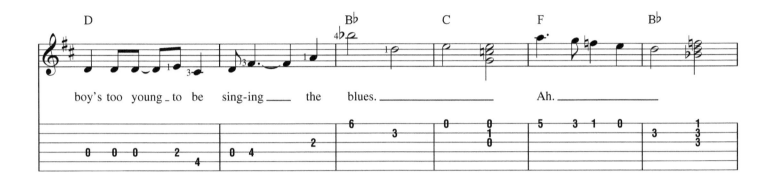

boy's too young ___ to be sing-ing ___ the blues. ___   Ah. ___

Chorus

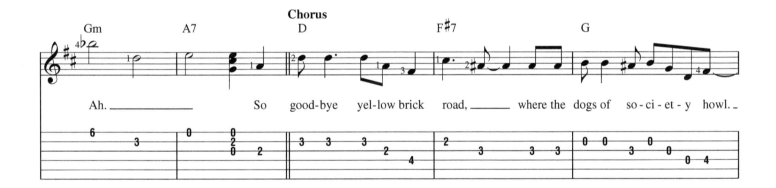

Ah. ___   So good-bye yel-low brick road, ___ where the dogs of so - ci - et - y howl. ___

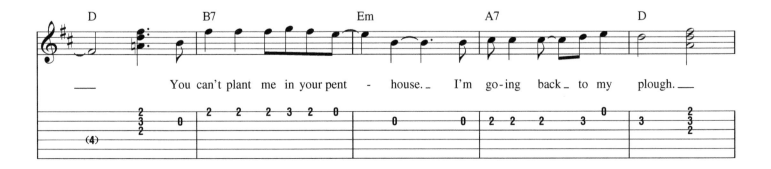

___ You can't plant me in your pent - house. ___ I'm go-ing back ___ to my plough. ___

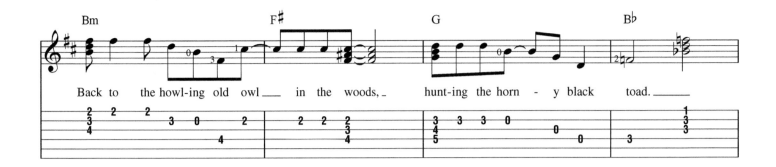

Back to the howl-ing old owl ___ in the woods, ___ hunt-ing the horn - y black toad. _____

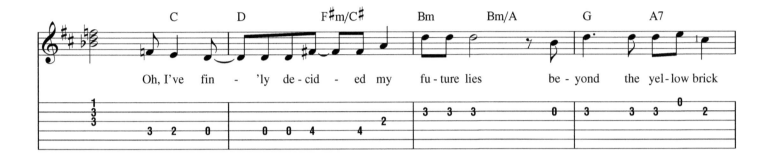

Oh, I've fin - 'ly de - cid - ed my fu - ture lies be - yond the yel - low brick

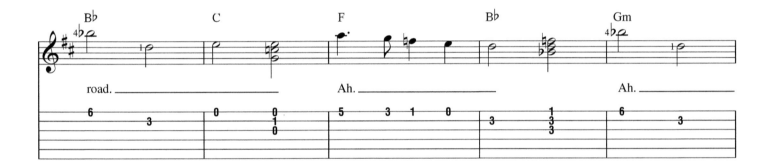

road. _____ Ah. _____ Ah. _____

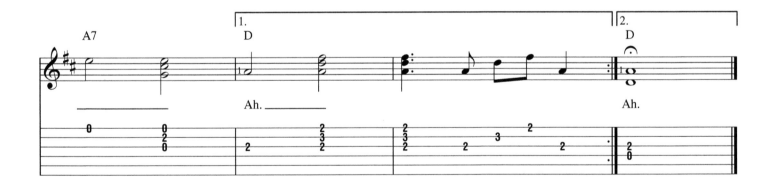

Ah. _____ Ah.

Additional Lyrics

2. What do you think you'll do then?
   I bet they shoot down your plane.
   It'll take you a couple of vodka and tonics
   To set you on your feet again.
   Maybe you'll get a replacement,
   There's plenty like me to be found.
   Mongrels who ain't got a penny,
   Sniffing for tidbits like you on the ground.

Candle in the Wind

Words and Music by Elton John and Bernie Taupin

*Capo II

Strum Pattern: 3
Pick Pattern: 2

Verse
Moderately

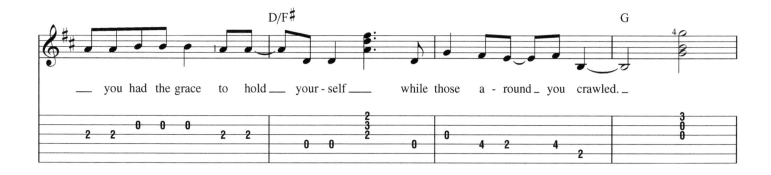

1. Good-bye, Nor - ma Jean. ___ Though I nev - er knew you ___ at all, ___
2., 3. *See additional lyrics*

*Opional: To match recording, place capo at 2nd fret.

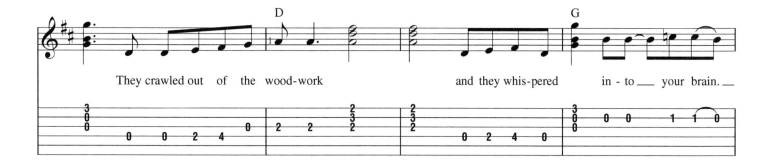

___ you had the grace to hold ___ your-self ___ while those a - round ___ you crawled. ___

They crawled out of the wood-work and they whis-pered in - to ___ your brain. ___

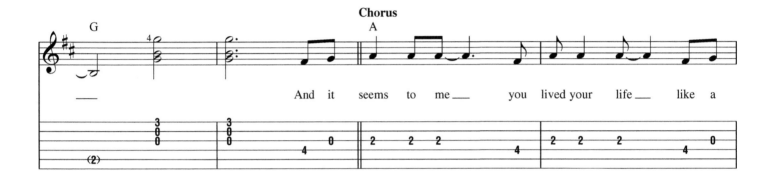

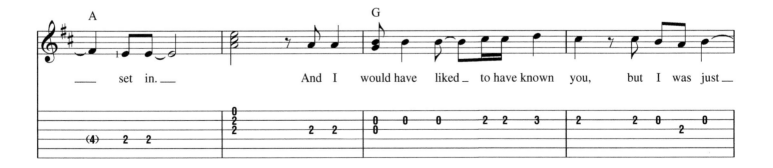

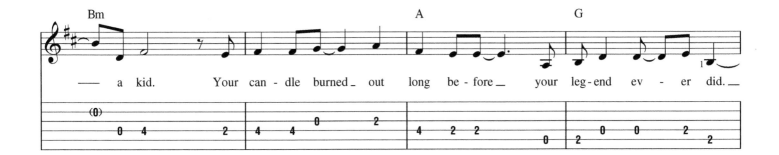

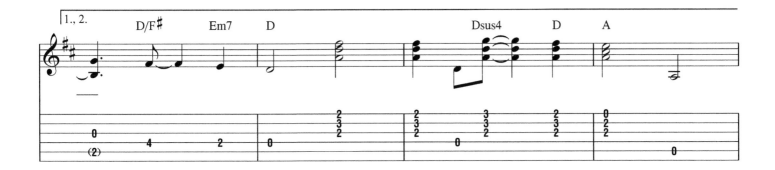

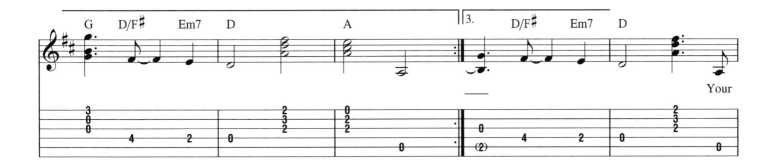

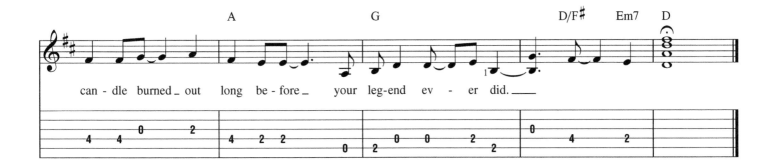

Additional Lyrics

2. Loneliness was tough, the toughest role you ever played.
   Hollywood created a superstar and pain was the price you paid.
   And even when you died, oh, the press still hounded you.
   All the papers had to say was that Marilyn was found in the nude.

3. Goodbye, Normaa Jean. Though I never knew you at all,
   You had the grace to hold yourself while those around you crawled.
   Goodbye, Norma Jean, from a young man in the twenty-second row,
   Who sees you as something more than sexual, more than just our Marilyn Monroe.

Bennie and the Jets

Words and Music by Elton John and Bernie Taupin

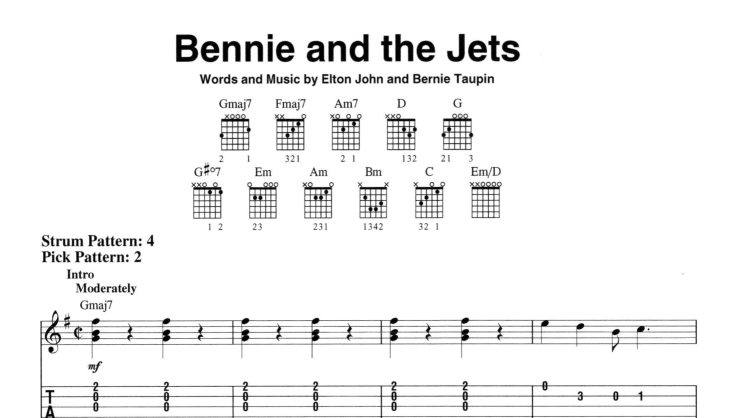

Strum Pattern: 4
Pick Pattern: 2

Intro
Moderately

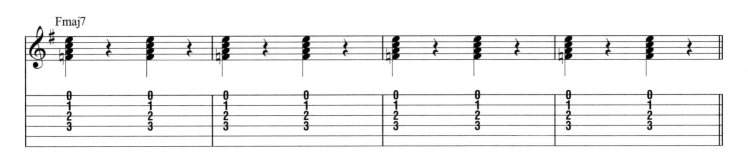

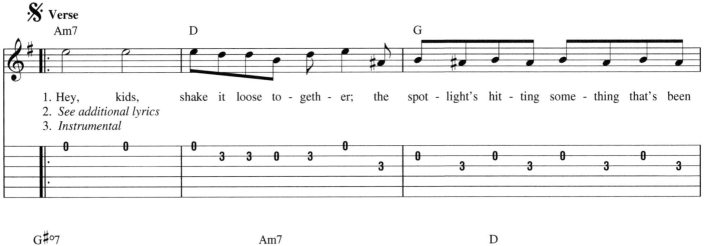

1. Hey, kids, shake it loose to - geth - er; the spot - light's hit - ting some - thing that's been
2. *See additional lyrics*
3. *Instrumental*

known to change the weath - er. We'll kill the fat - ted calf __ to - night, __ so stick a -

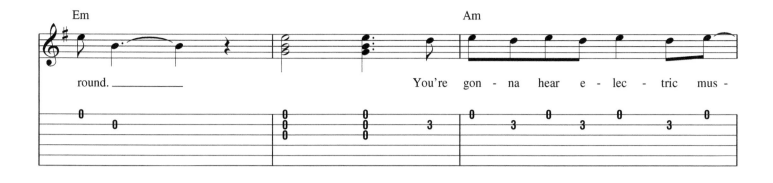

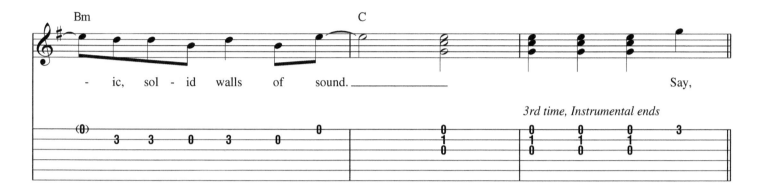

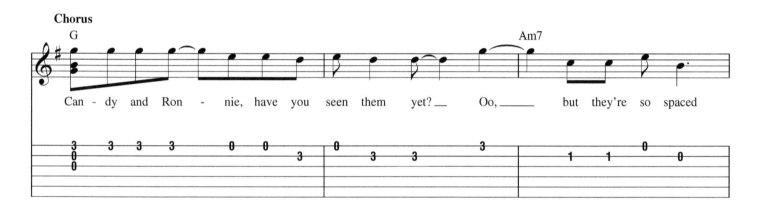

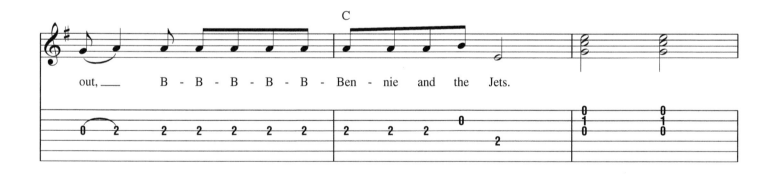

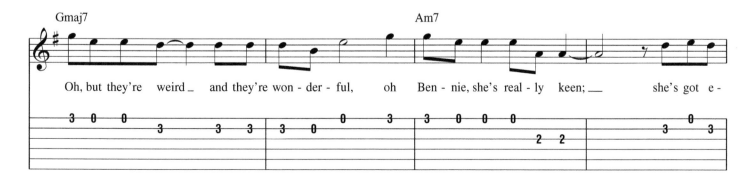

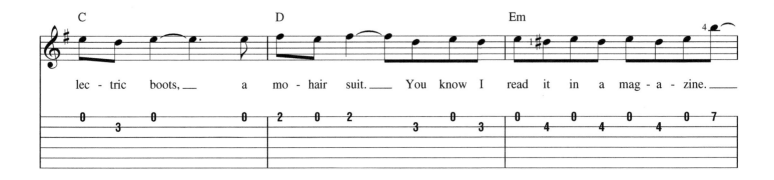

lec - tric boots, __ a mo - hair suit. __ You know I read it in a mag - a - zine. __

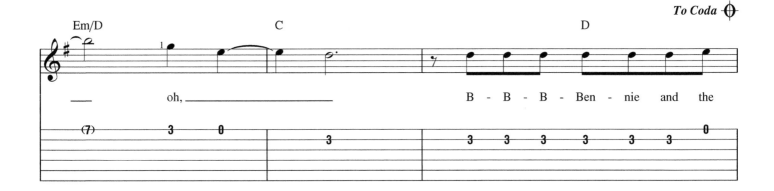

To Coda ⊕

— oh, __ B - B - B - Ben - nie and the

Jets.

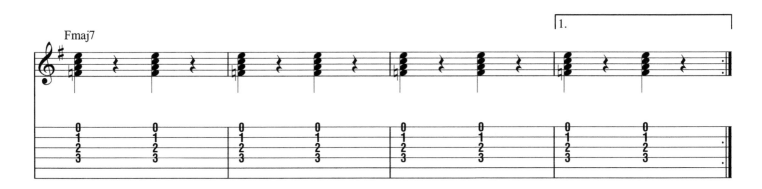

1.

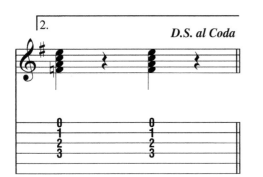

2.

D.S. al Coda

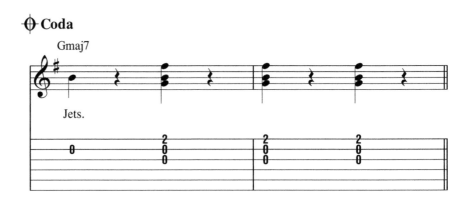

⊕ Coda

Jets.

Outro

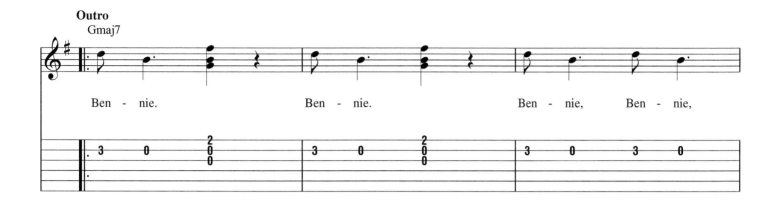

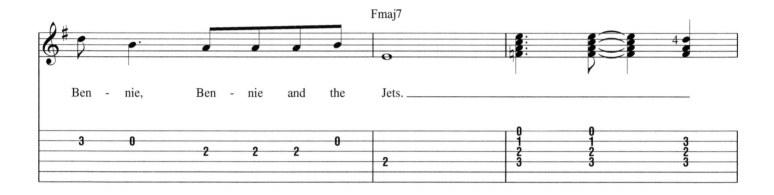

Repeat and fade

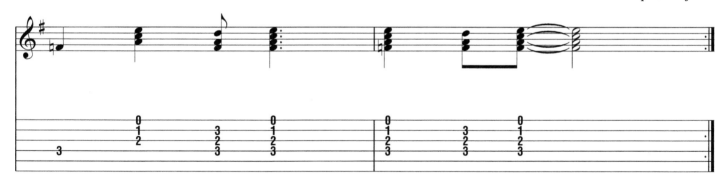

Additional Lyrics

2. Hey, kids, plug into the faithless,
   Maybe they're blinded, but Bennie makes them ageless.
   We shall survive; let us take ourselves along
   Where we fight our parents out in the streets
   To find who's right and who's wrong.

Don't Let the Sun Go Down on Me

Words and Music by Elton John and Bernie Taupin

Strum Pattern: 3, 4
Pick Pattern: 5

1. I can't light no more of your dark - ness. __

All my pic - tures _____ seem to fade _ to black _ and white. _

I'm grow - in' tired, and time stands still be - fore _____ me,

fro-zen here __ on the lad - der of my __ life. __

Too late __ to save my-self from fall - ing.

I took a chance and changed your way __ of life, __

Harm.- - - - - - - - - - - -

Pitch: B G B

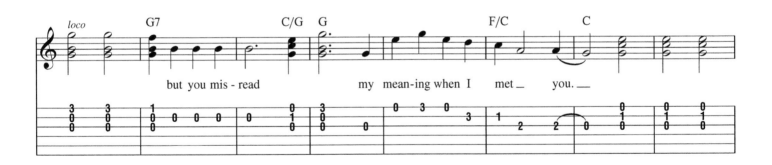

but you mis - read my mean-ing when I met __ you. __

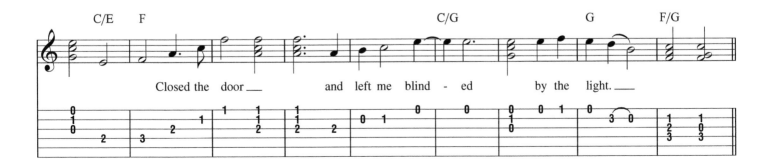

Closed the door __ and left me blind - ed by the light. __

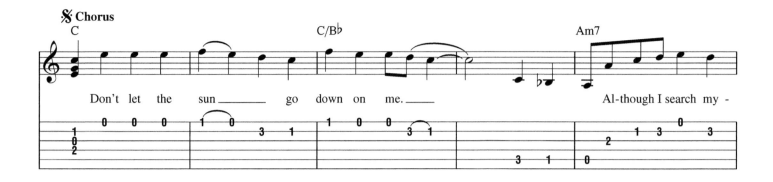

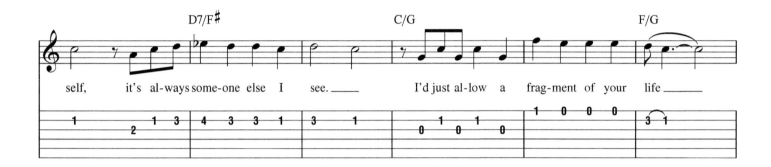

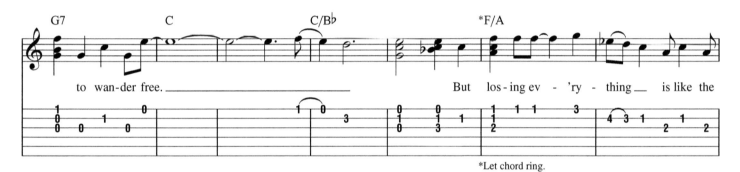

*Let chord ring.

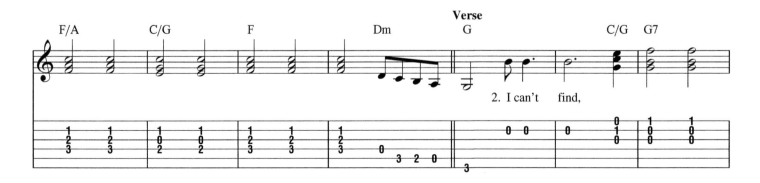

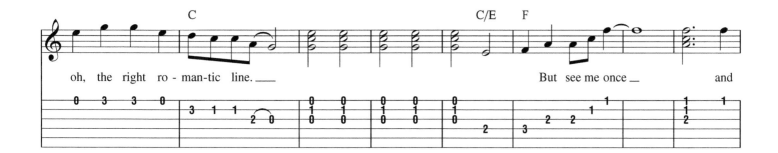

oh, the right ro - man - tic line. ___ But see me once ___ and

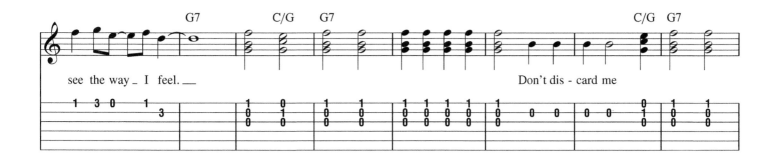

see the way ___ I feel. ___ Don't dis - card me

just be - cause ___ you think ___ I mean ___ you harm. _____ But these cuts ___

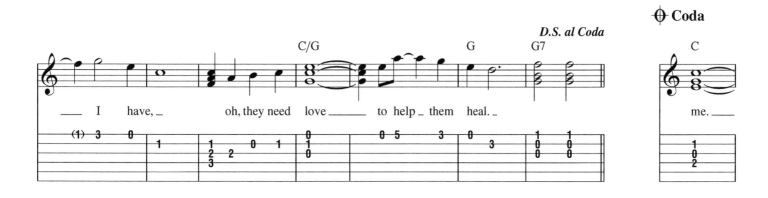

___ I have, ___ oh, they need love _____ to help ___ them heal. ___ me. ___

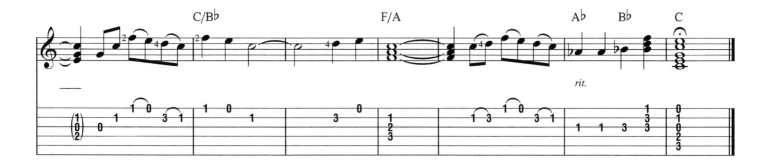

The Bitch Is Back

Words and Music by Elton John and Bernie Taupin

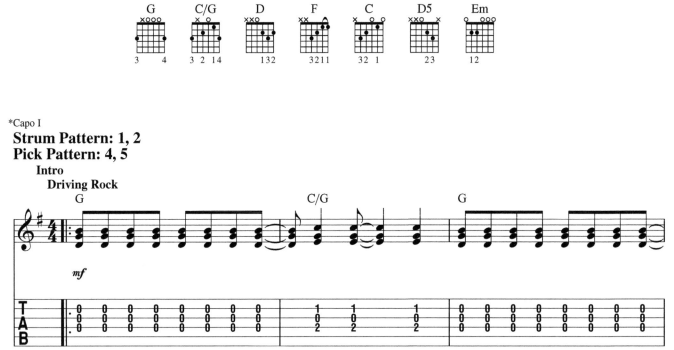

*Capo I

Strum Pattern: 1, 2
Pick Pattern: 4, 5

Intro
Driving Rock

*Optional: To match recording, place capo at 1st fret.

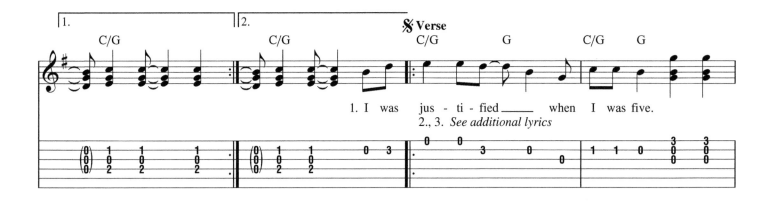

1. I was jus - ti - fied ___ when I was five.
2., 3. *See additional lyrics*

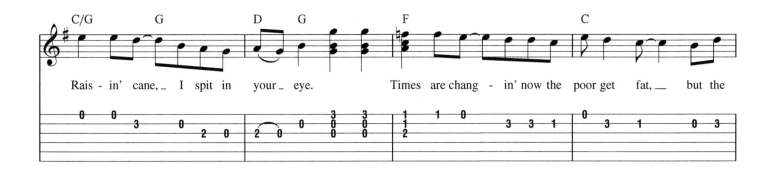

Rais - in' cane, _ I spit in your _ eye. Times are chang - in' now the poor get fat, _ but the

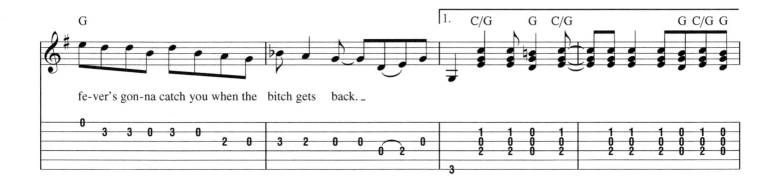

fe-ver's gon-na catch you when the bitch gets back. _

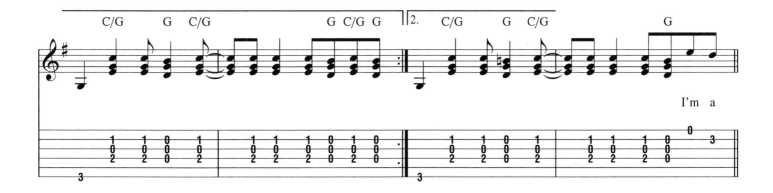

I'm a

Chorus

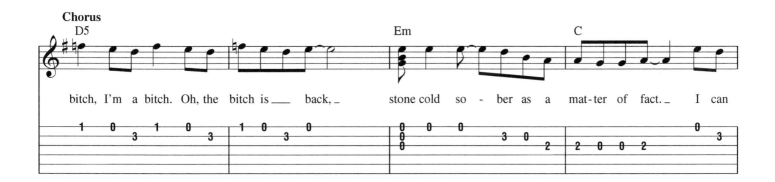

bitch, I'm a bitch. Oh, the bitch is __ back, _ stone cold so - ber as a mat-ter of fact. _ I can

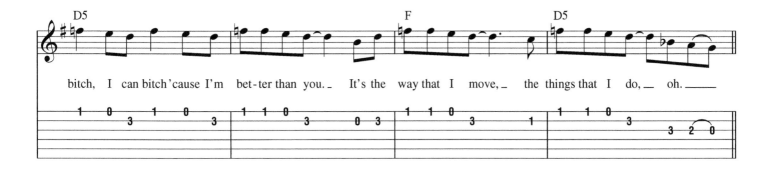

bitch, I can bitch 'cause I'm bet-ter than you. _ It's the way that I move, _ the things that I do, _ oh. ___

Interlude

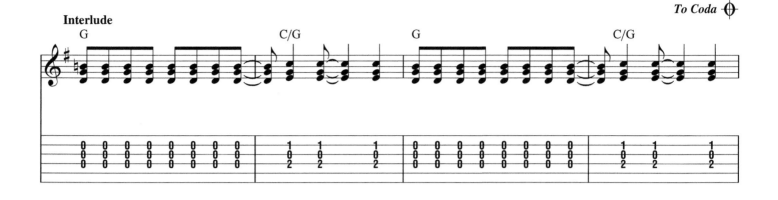

D.S. al Coda
(take 2nd ending)

3. I

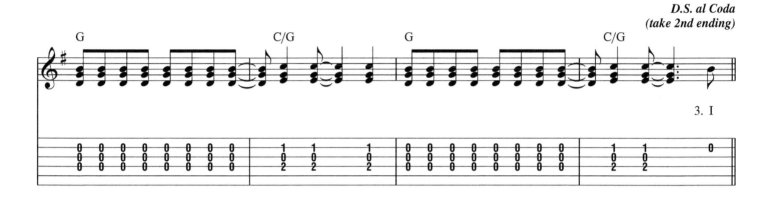

⊕ **Coda**
Outro

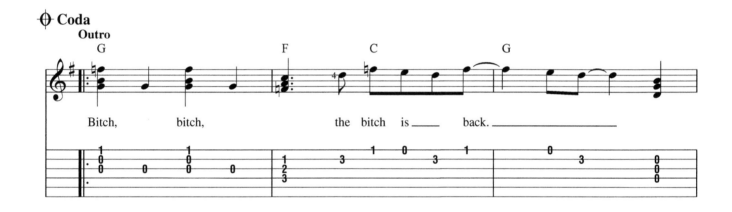

Bitch,   bitch,   the bitch is ____ back. _____

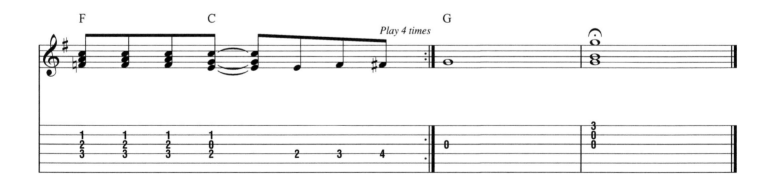

Additional Lyrics

2. Eat meat on Friday, that's alright.
   I even like steak on a Saturday night.
   I can bitch the best at your social do's.
   I get high in the evening sniffing pots of glue.

3. I entertain by picking brains,
   Sell my soul by dropping names.
   I don't like those! My God, what's that!
   Oh, it's full of nasty habits when the bitch bets back.

Someone Saved My Life Tonight

Words and Music by Elton John and Bernie Taupin

*Capo I

Strum Pattern: 4
Pick Pattern: 5

Intro
Slowly

*Optional: To match recording, place capo at 1st fret.

Verse

1. When I think of those east end lights, mug-gy nights, the cur-tains drawn in the
2. *See additional lyrics*

lit-tle room down-stairs,_ pri-ma-don-na, Lord, you real-ly should have been there,

*Use Pattern 10

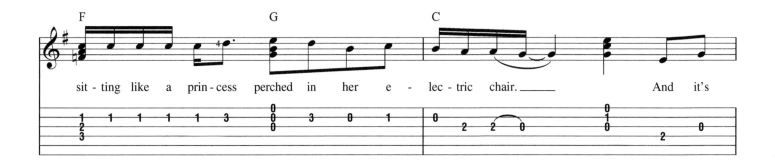

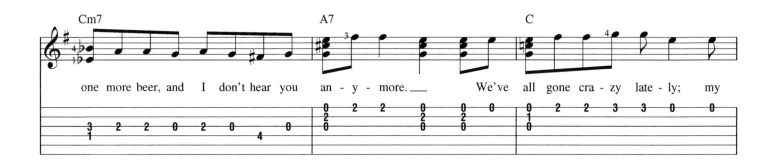

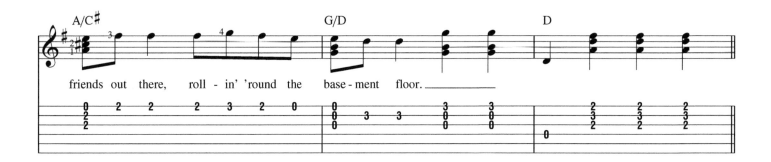

% Chorus

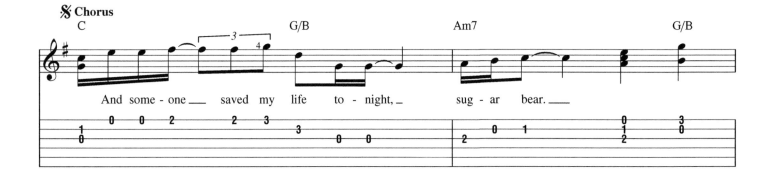

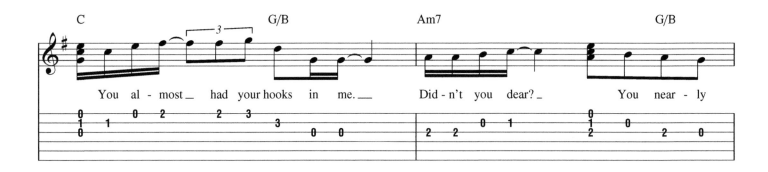

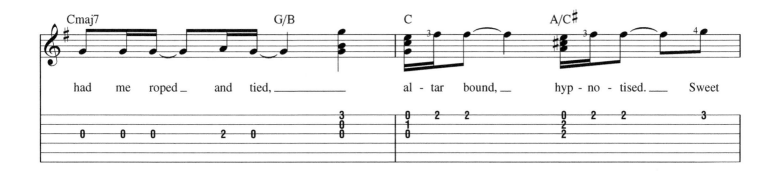

had me roped __ and tied, _____ al - tar bound, __ hyp - no - tised. __ Sweet

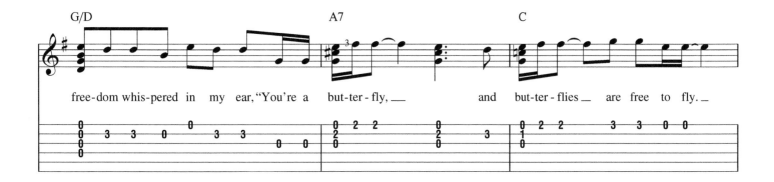

free-dom whis-pered in my ear, "You're a but-ter-fly, ___ and but-ter-flies __ are free to fly. __

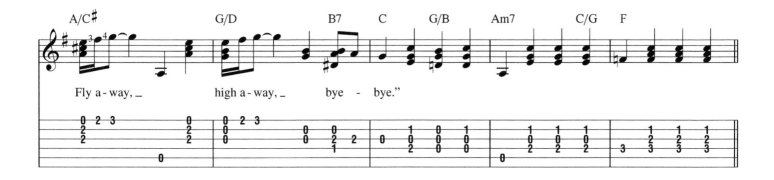

Fly a - way, _ high a - way, _ bye - bye."

Interlude

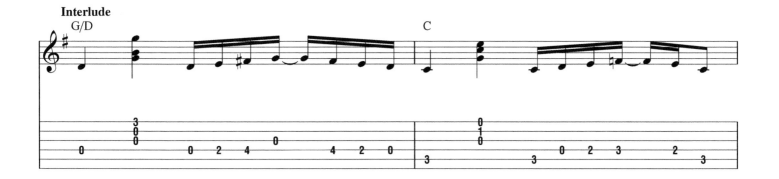

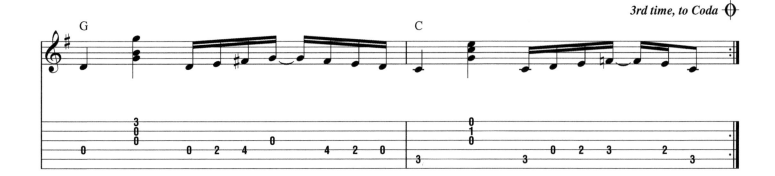

Bridge

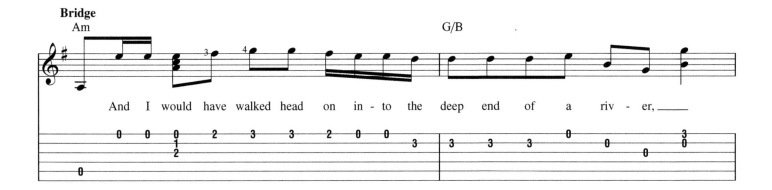

And I would have walked head on in-to the deep end of a riv - er, ____

cling-ing to your stocks and bonds, __ pay - ing your H. P. de-mands for - ev - er. ____

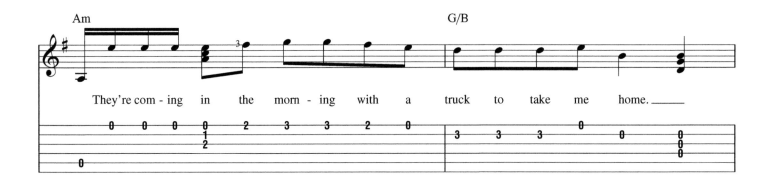

They're com - ing in the morn - ing with a truck to take me home. ____

Some-one saved my life to-night.____ Some-one saved my life to-night.____

Some-one saved my life to-night.____ Some-one saved my life to-night.____

D.S. al Coda

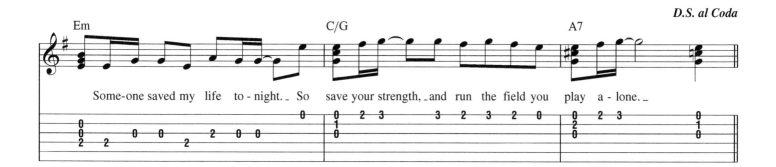

Some-one saved my life to-night.____ So save your strength, __and run the field you play a - lone. __

⊕ **Coda**

Repeat and fade

Outro

Some-one saved, some-one saved, some-one saved my life to - night. __

Additional Lyrics

2. I never realized the passing hours
   Of evening showers,
   A slip noose hanging in my darkest dreams.
   I'm strangled by your haunted social scene,
   Just a pawn out-played by a dominating queen.
   It's four o'clock in the morning.
   Damn it!
   Listen to me good.
   I'm sleeping with myself tonight.
   Saved in time, thank God my music's still alive.

Philadelphia Freedom

Words and Music by Elton John and Bernie Taupin

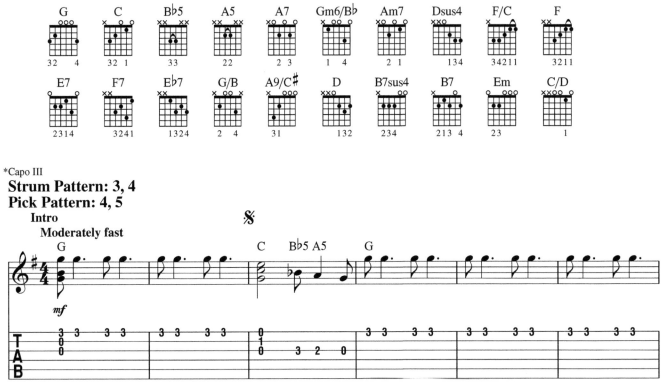

*Capo III

Strum Pattern: 3, 4
Pick Pattern: 4, 5

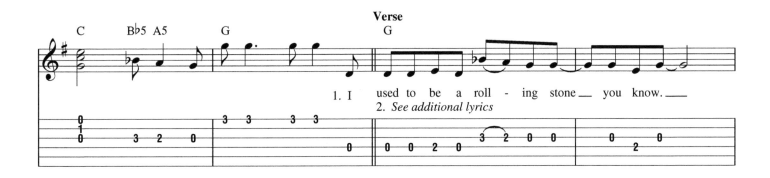

*Optional: To match recording, place capo at 3rd fret.

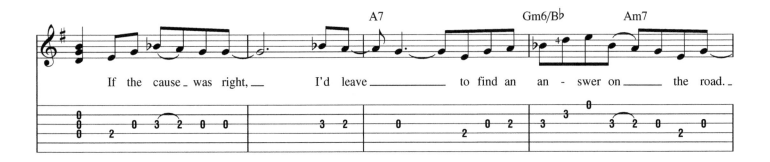

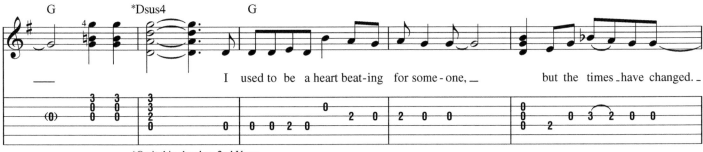

*Omit this chord on 2nd Verse.

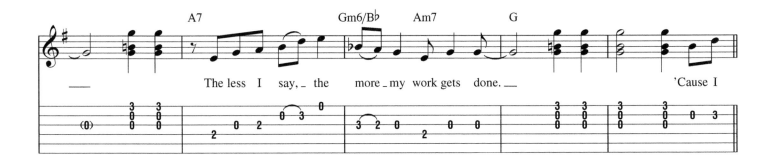

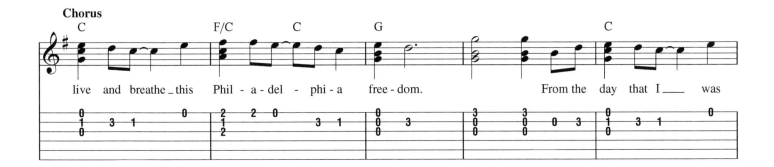

Chorus

Oh, Phil - a - del - phi - a free - dom shine on

me. _____ I love __ ya. Shine the light _____ through the eyes __ of the one _ left be -

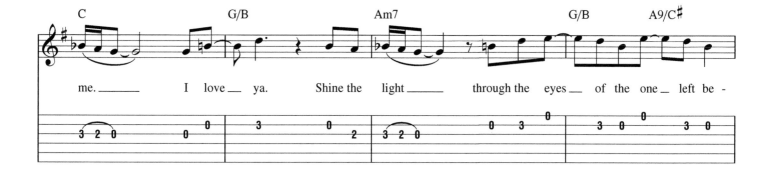

hind. _____ Shine the light, _ shine _ the light. Shine the light, _ won't you

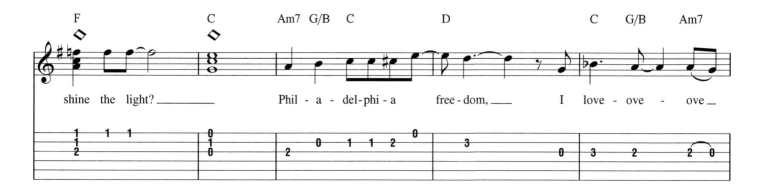

shine the light? _____ Phil - a - del - phi - a free - dom, ____ I love - ove - ove _

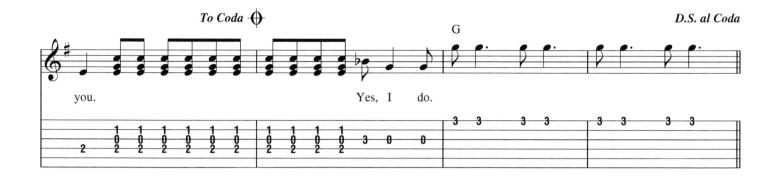

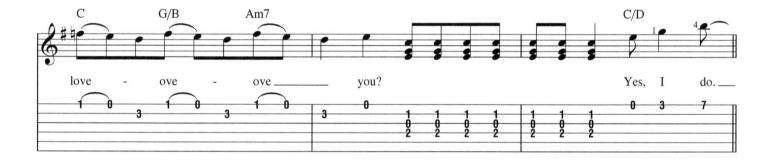

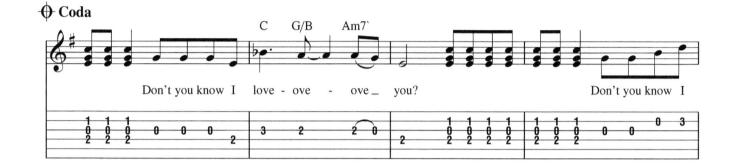

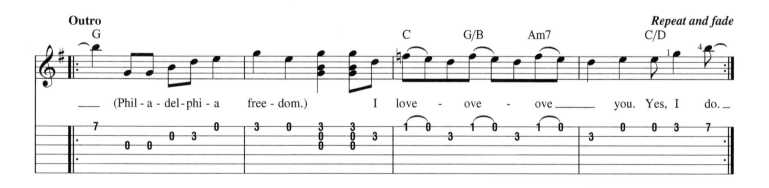

Additional Lyrics

2. If you choose to, you can live your life alone.
   Some people choose the city,
   Some others choose the good old family home.
   I like living easy without family ties,
   'Til the whippoorwill of freedom zapped me
   Right between the eyes.

Island Girl

Words and Music by Elton John and Bernie Taupin

*Capo V

Strum Pattern: 3, 6
Pick Pattern: 3, 5

Intro
Moderately fast

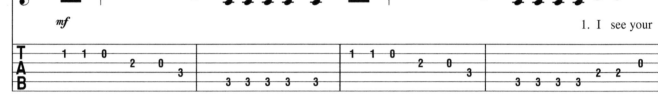

1. I see your

*Optional: To match recording, place capo at 5th fret.

Verse

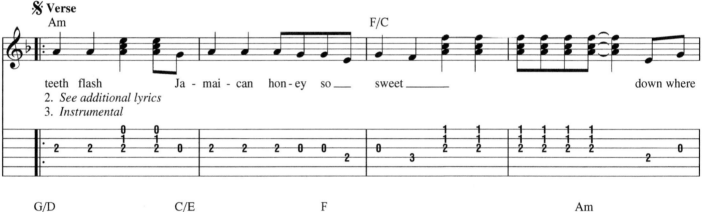

teeth flash Ja - mai - can hon - ey so ___ sweet _____ down where
2. *See additional lyrics*
3. *Instrumental*

Lex - ing - ton ___ cross for - ty sev - enth street. _ Oh, she's a big girl,

she's stand-ing six foot three, _ turn-ing tricks for the dudes in the

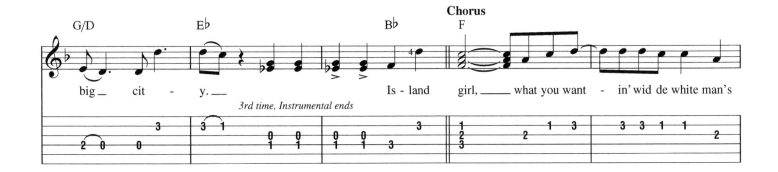

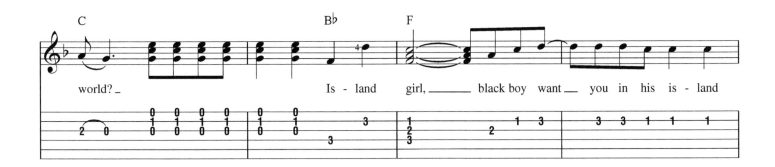

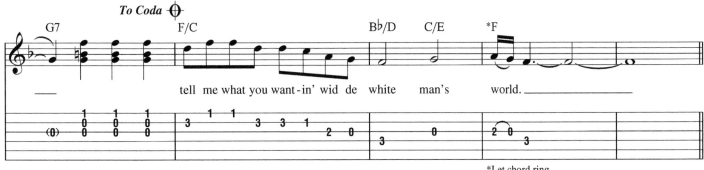

*Let chord ring.

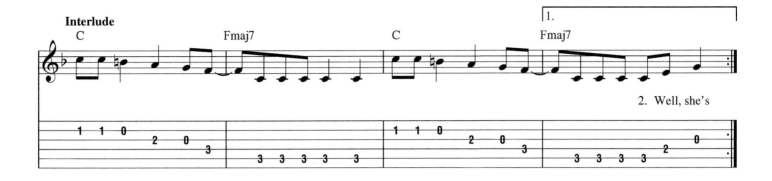

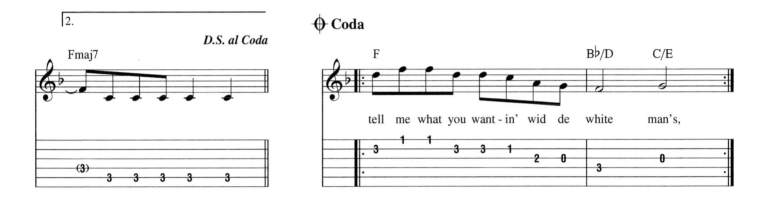

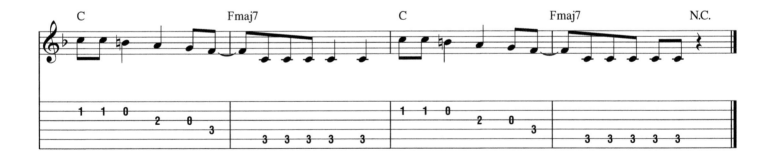

Additional Lyrics

2. Well, she's black as coal
But she burn like a fire,
And she wrap herself around you
Like a well-worn tire.
You feel her nail scratch your back
Just like a rake.
Oh, he one more gone,
He one more john who make de mistake.

Sorry Seems to Be the Hardest Word

Words and Music by Elton John and Bernie Taupin

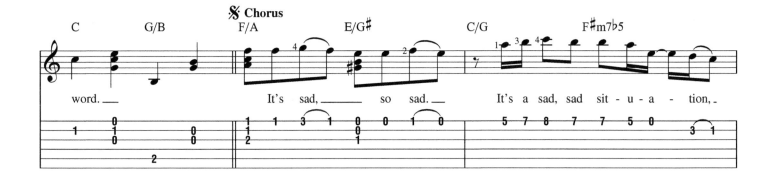

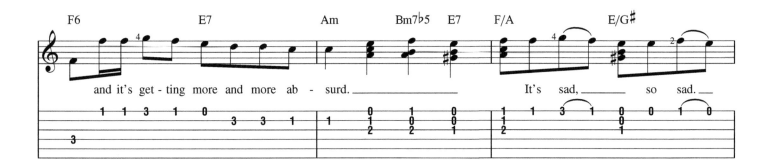

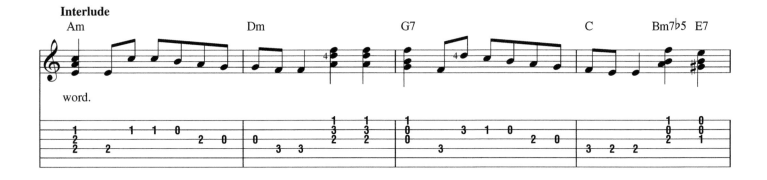

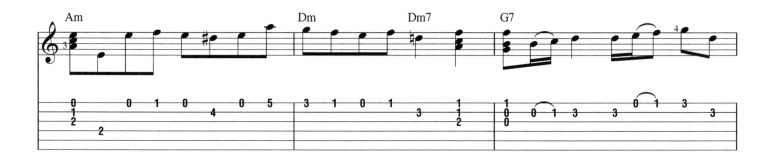

⊕ Coda

D.S. al Coda

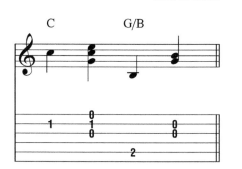

Outro-Verse

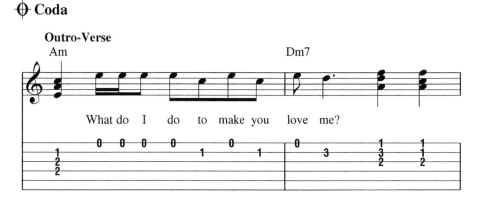

What do I do to make you love me?

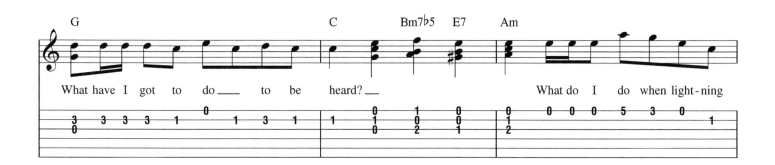

What have I got to do ___ to be heard? ___ What do I do when light-ning

strikes me? What have I got to do, ___ what have I got to do? ___

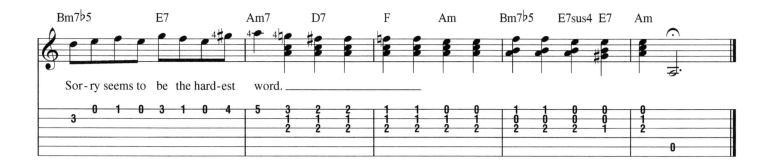

Sor-ry seems to be the hard-est word. ___

Don't Go Breaking My Heart

Words and Music by Carte Blanche and Ann Orson

*Optional: To match recording, tune down 1 step.

**Sung one octave higher throughout.

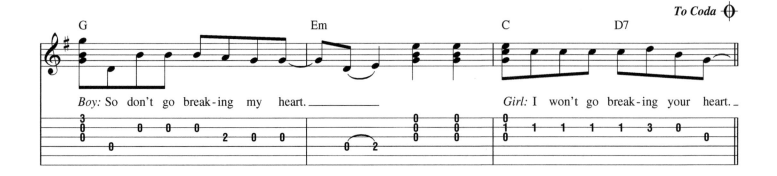

Boy: So don't go break-ing my heart. _____   Girl: I won't go break-ing your heart. _

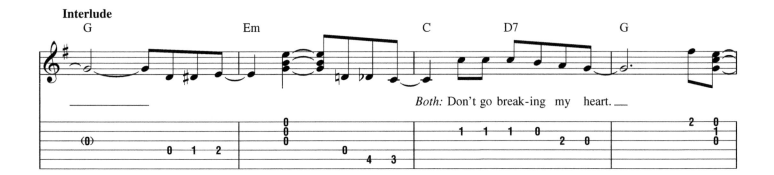

Interlude

Both: Don't go break-ing my heart. _

⊕ **Coda**

D.S. al Coda

Outro

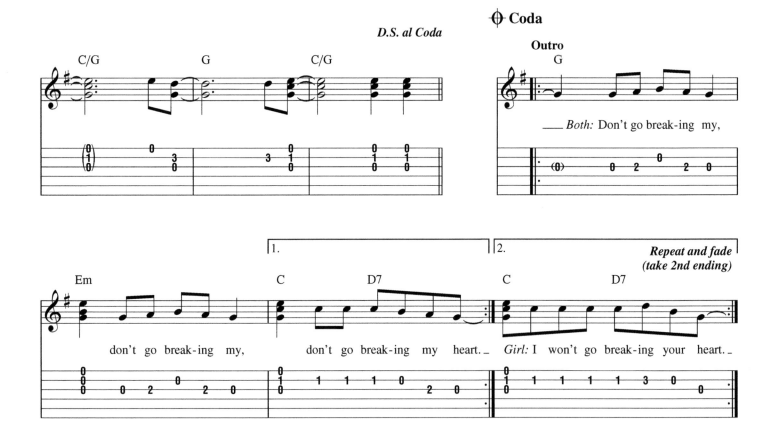

_____ Both: Don't go break-ing my,

1.

2.

Repeat and fade
(take 2nd ending)

don't go break-ing my,   don't go break-ing my heart. _   Girl: I won't go break-ing your heart. _

Additional Lyrics

2. *Boy:* And nobody told us.
   Girl: 'Cause nobody showed us.
   Boy: And now it's up to us, babe.
   Girl: Oh, I think we can make it.
   Boy: So don't misunderstand me.
   Girl: You put the light in my life.
   Boy: Oh, you put the spark to the flame.
   Girl: I've got your heart in my sights.

Little Jeannie

Words and Music by Elton John and Gary Osborne

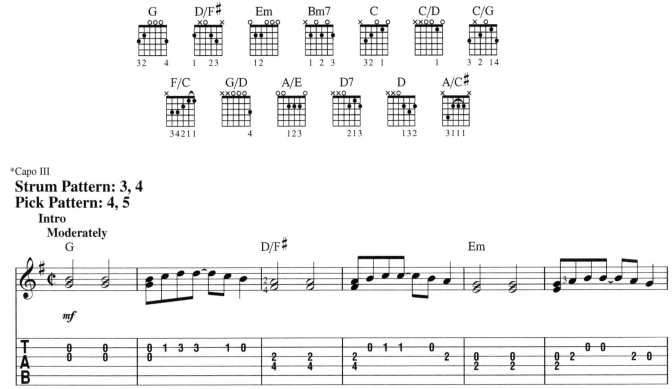

*Capo III

Strum Pattern: 3, 4
Pick Pattern: 4, 5

Intro
Moderately

*Optional: To match recording, place capo at 3rd fret.

Verse

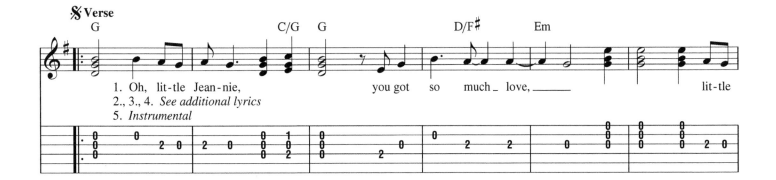

1. Oh, lit-tle Jean-nie,   you got   so   much   love,   lit-tle
2., 3., 4. *See additional lyrics*
5. *Instrumental*

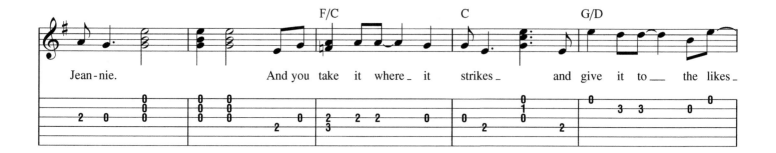

Jean-nie. And you take it where it strikes and give it to the likes

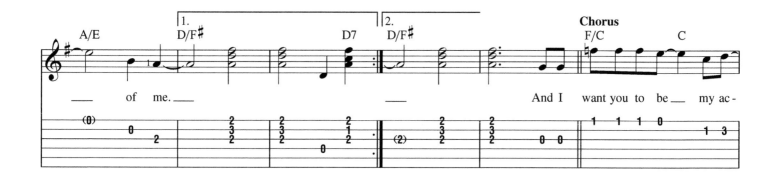

of me. And I want you to be my ac-

-ro-bat. I want you to be my lov-

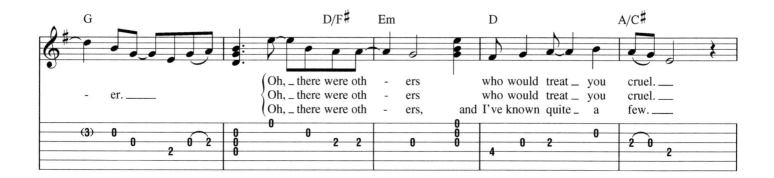

-er. Oh, there were oth - ers who would treat you cruel.
Oh, there were oth - ers who would treat you cruel.
Oh, there were oth - ers, and I've known quite a few.

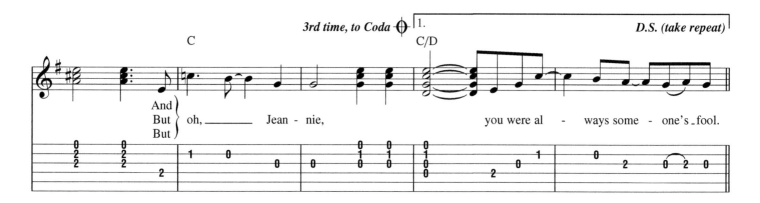

And
But oh, Jean - nie, you were al - ways some - one's fool.
But

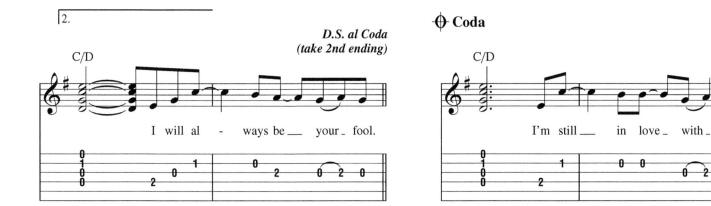

Outro

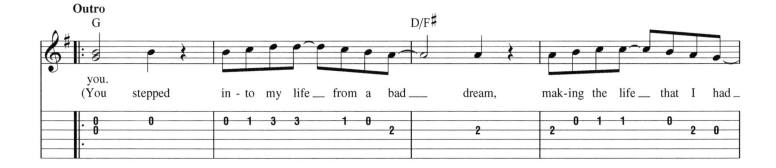

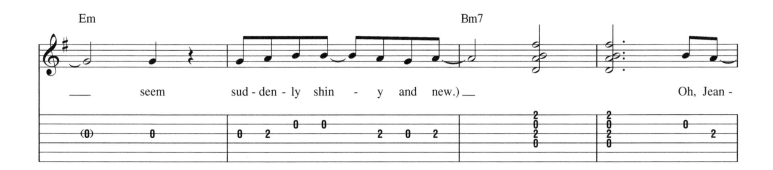

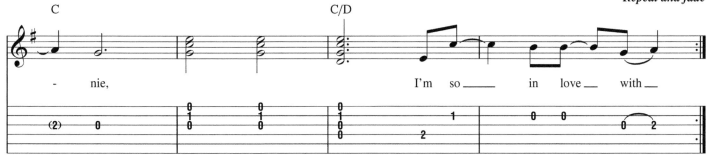

Additional Lyrics

2. Oh, little Jeannie,
   She got so much love, little Jeannie.
   So I see you when I can.
   You make me all a man can be.

3. Little Jeannie,
   You got so much time, little Jeannie.
   Though you've grown beyond your years,
   You still retain the fears of youth.

4. Oh, little Jeannie,
   You got so much time, little Jeannie.
   But you're burning it up so fast,
   Searching for some lasting truth.

I'm Still Standing

Words and Music by Elton John and Bernie Taupin

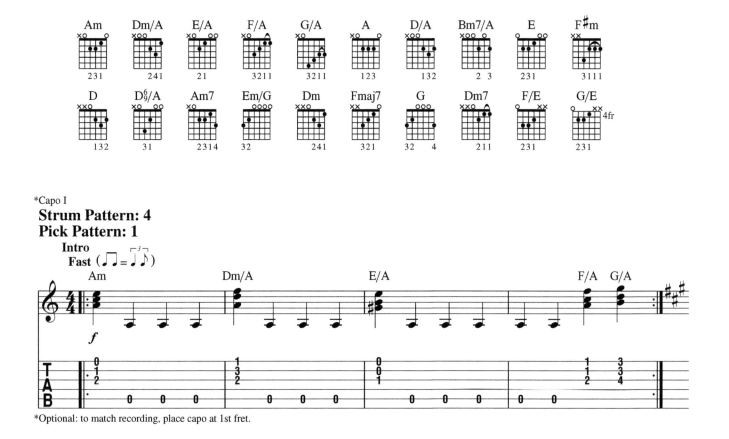

*Capo I

Strum Pattern: 4
Pick Pattern: 1

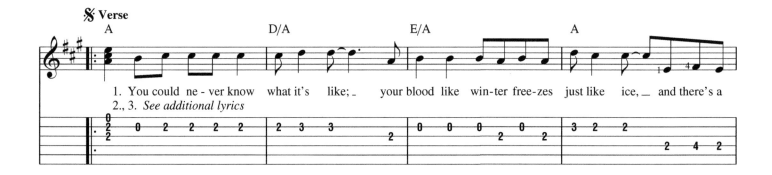

*Optional: to match recording, place capo at 1st fret.

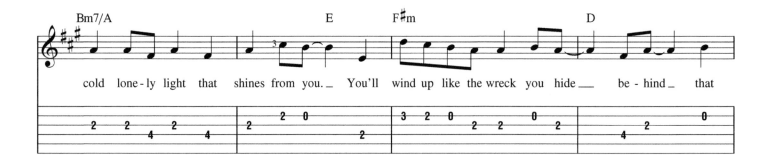

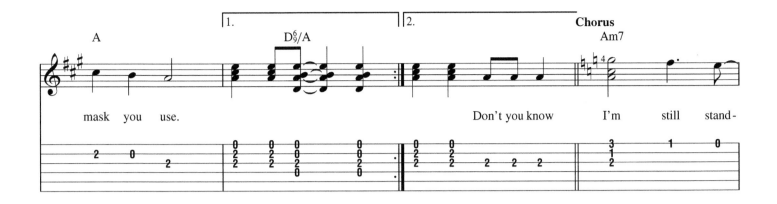

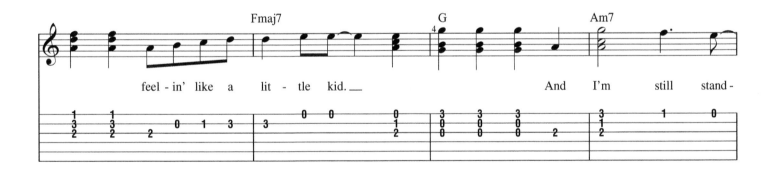

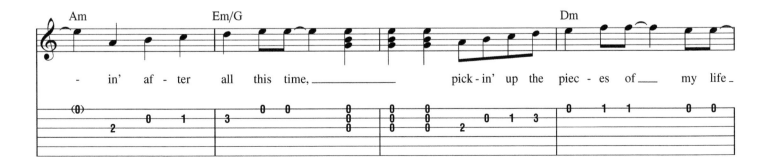

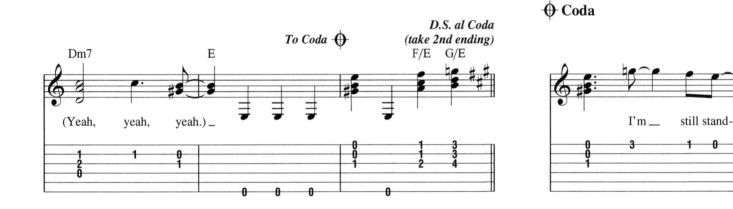

Additional Lyrics

2. And did you think this fool could ever win?
   Well, look at me, I'm comin' back again.
   I got a taste of love in a simple way,
   And if you need to know, while I'm still standin'
   You just fade away.

3. Once I never could hope to win,
   You startin' down the road and leavin' me again.
   The threats you made were meant to cut me down,
   And if our love was just a circus,
   You'd be a clown by now.

I Guess That's Why They Call It the Blues

Words and Music by Elton John, Bernie Taupin and Davey Johnstone

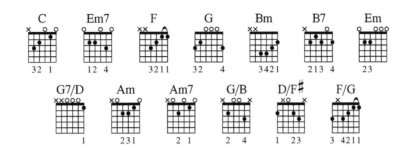

Strum Pattern: 1, 3
Pick Pattern: 3, 5

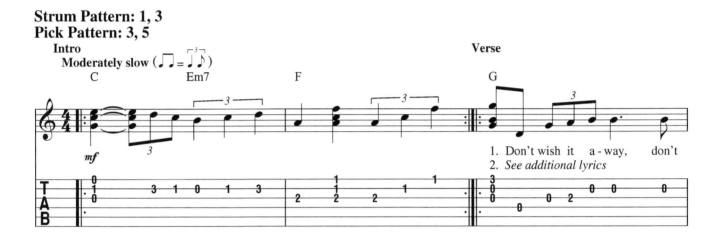

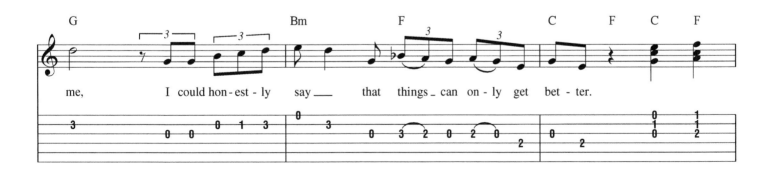

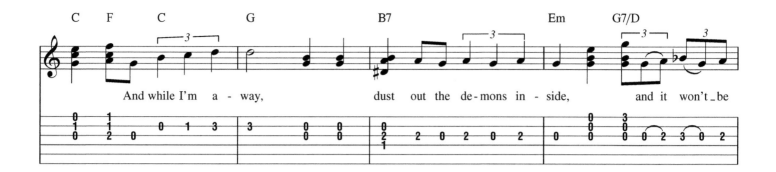

And while I'm a-way, dust out the de-mons in-side, and it won't _ be

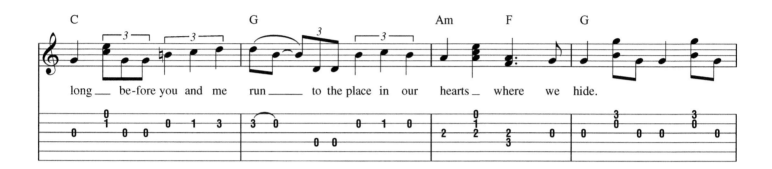

long __ be-fore you and me run _____ to the place in our hearts _ where we hide.

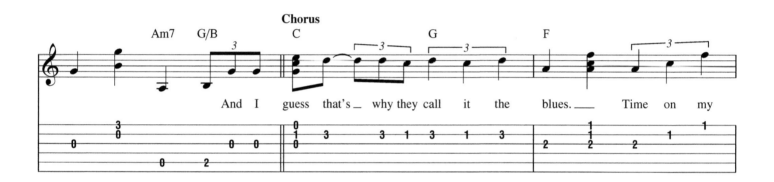

Chorus

And I guess that's _ why they call it the blues. __ Time on my

hands __ could be time spent with you, __ laugh-ing like chil-dren, liv-ing like lov-ers, roll-ing like

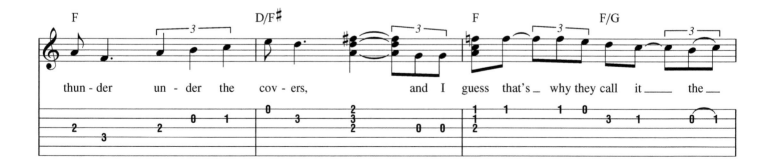

thun-der un-der the cov-ers, and I guess that's _ why they call it _____ the _

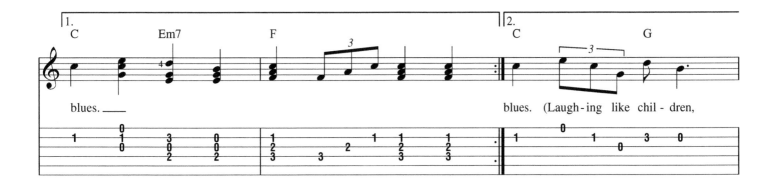

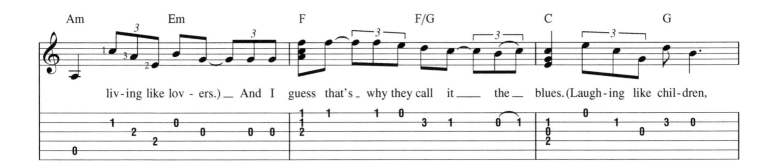

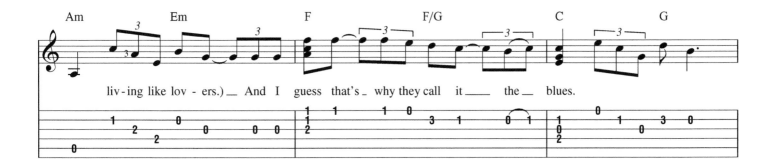

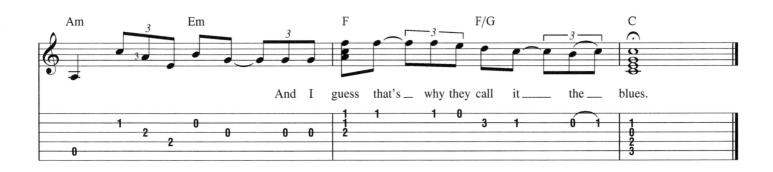

Additional Lyrics

2. Just stare into space;
   Picture my face in your hands.
   Live for each second without hesitation
   And never forget I'm your man.
   Wait on me, girl, cry in the night if it helps,
   But more than ever I simply love you
   More than I love life in itself.

Sad Songs (Say So Much)

Words and Music by Elton John and Bernie Taupin

Strum Pattern: 4
Pick Pattern: 4

Intro
Moderately

*Omit tie on repeat.

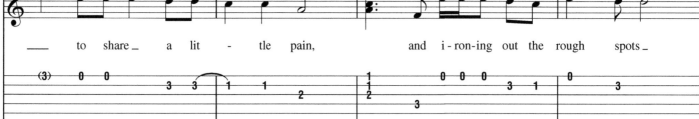

1. Guess there are times __ when we __ all __ need __ to share __ a lit-tle pain, and i-ron-ing out the rough spots __
2. *See additional lyrics*

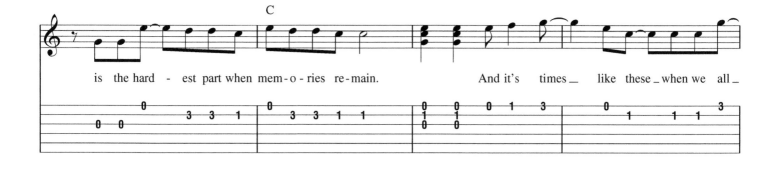

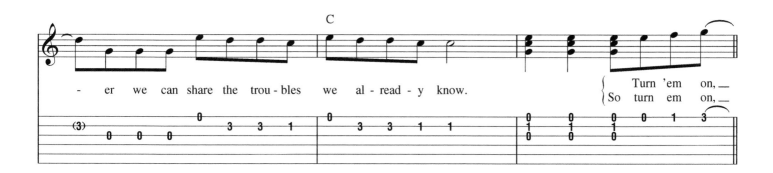

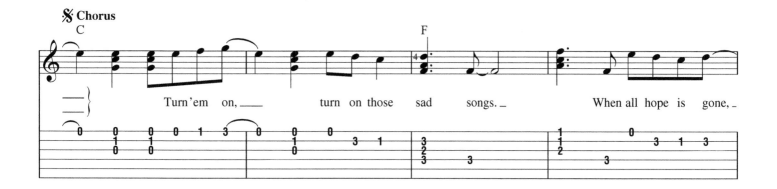

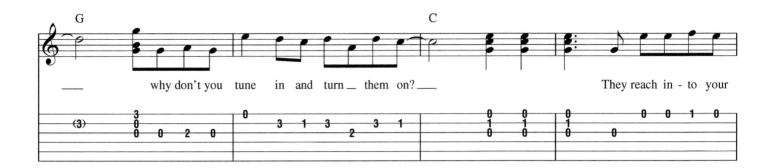

why don't you tune in and turn _ them on? ___ They reach in - to your

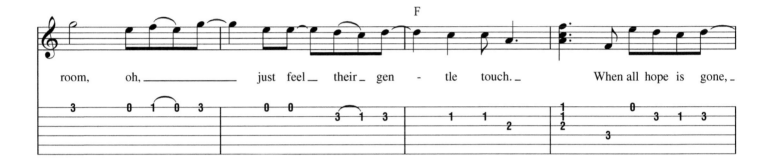

room, oh, _____ just feel _ their _ gen - tle touch. _ When all hope is gone, _

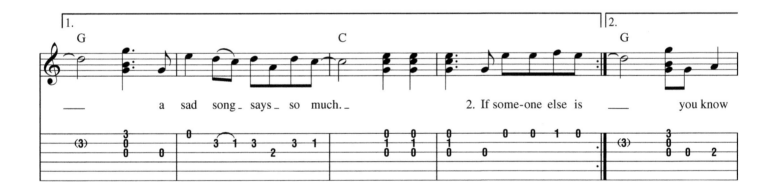

a sad song _ says _ so much. _ 2. If some-one else is ___ you know

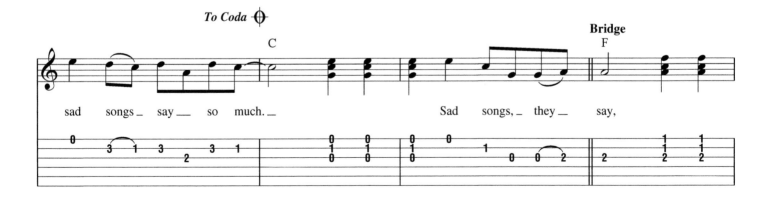

sad songs _ say _ so much. _ Sad songs, _ they _ say,

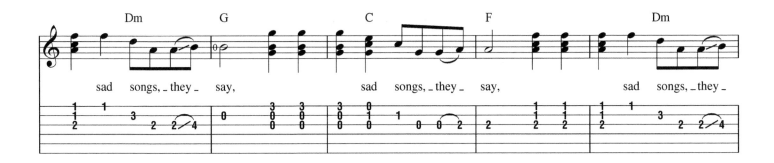

sad   songs, _ they _ say,   sad   songs, _ they _ say,   sad   songs, _ they

⊕ Coda

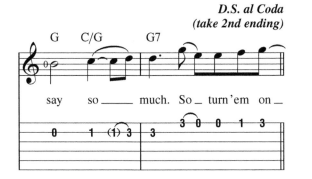

D.S. al Coda
(take 2nd ending)

say   so ____ much. So _ turn 'em on _

Outro

____   When all hope is gone, _   you know

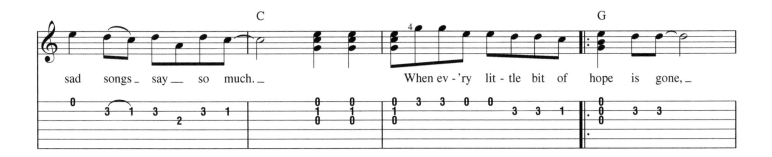

sad   songs _ say _ so   much. _   When ev - 'ry lit - tle bit of   hope   is   gone, _

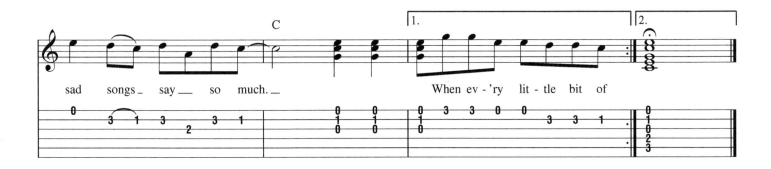

sad   songs _ say ___ so   much. _   When ev - 'ry lit - tle bit of

Additional Lyrics

2. If someone is sufferin' enough
   Oh, to write it down
   When ev'ry single word makes sense,
   Then it's easier to have those songs around.
   The kick inside is in the line
   That finally gets to you.
   And it feels so good to hurt so bad
   And suffer just enough to sing the blues.

I Don't Wanna Go On With You Like That

Words and Music by Elton John and Bernie Taupin

Strum Pattern: 3, 4
Pick Pattern: 4, 5

Intro
Moderately fast

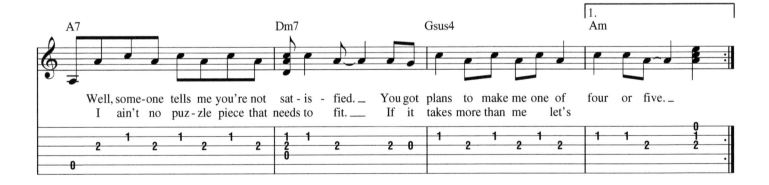

1. I've al-ways said that one's e-nough to love. ___ Now I hear you're brag-gin' one is not e-nough. ___
2. I guess this kind of thing's just in your blood. ___ But you won't catch ___ me count-ing up my love. ___
3. *See additional lyrics*

Well, some-one tells me you're not sat-is-fied. ___ You got plans to make me one of four or five. ___
I ain't no puz-zle piece that needs to fit. ___ If it takes more than me let's

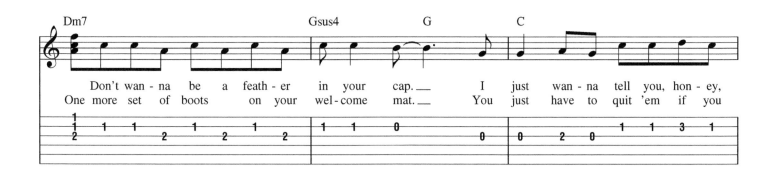

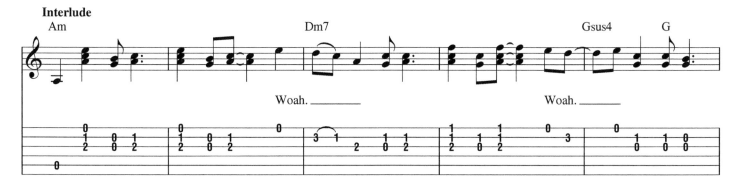

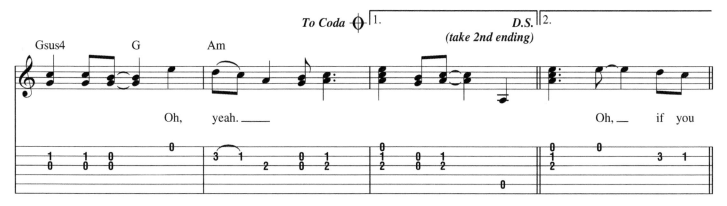

Bridge

wan-na spread it a-round, sis-ter, that's just fine, _ but I don't want a sec-ond hand-er feed-ing me lines. _ If you

D.S.S. al Coda

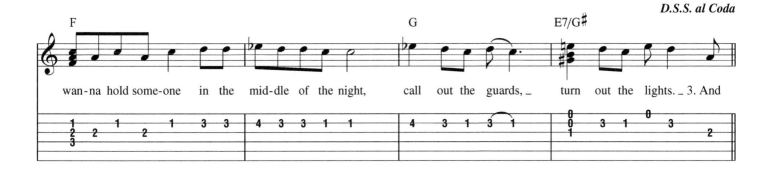

wan-na hold some-one in the mid-dle of the night, call out the guards, _ turn out the lights. _ 3. And

⊕ Coda

Outro

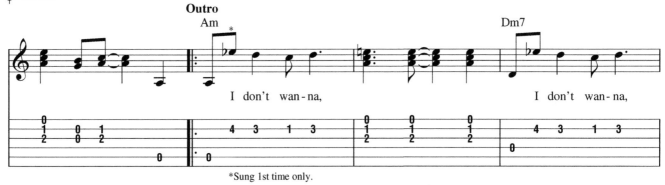

I don't wan-na, I don't wan-na,

*Sung 1st time only.

Repeat and fade

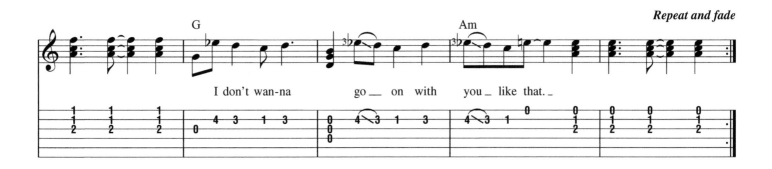

I don't wan-na go _ on with you _ like that. _

Additional Lyrics

3. It gets so hard sometimes to understand.
   This vicious circle's getting out of hand.
   Don't need an extra eye to see
   That the fire spreads faster in a breeze.

Nikita

Words and Music by Elton John and Bernie Taupin

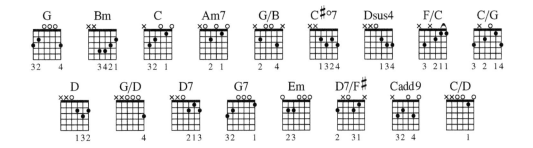

Strum Pattern: 4, 6
Pick Pattern: 5

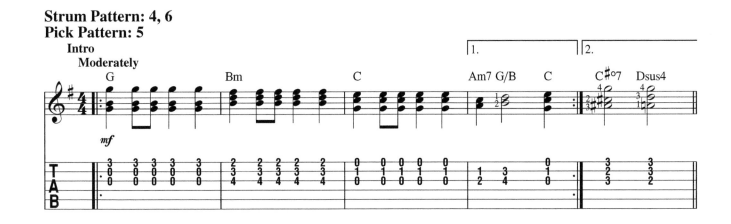

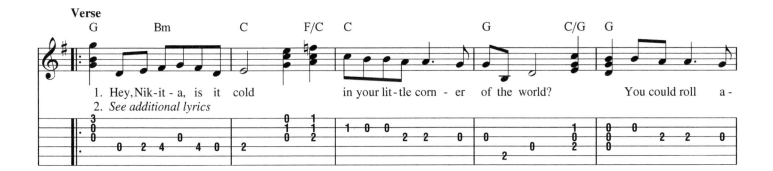

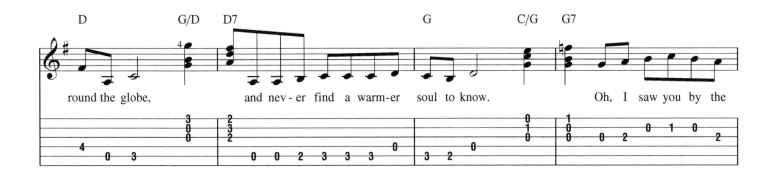

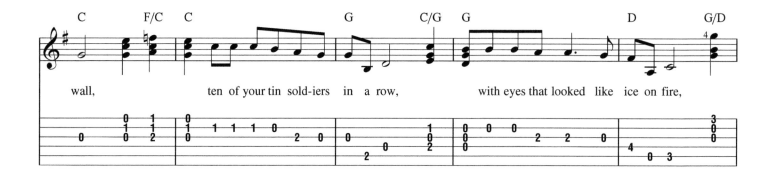

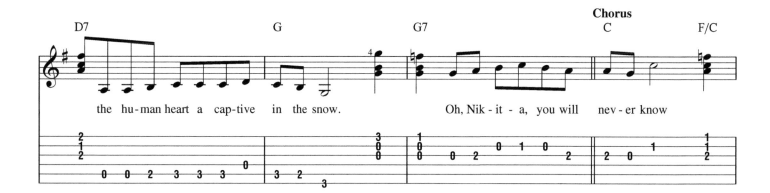

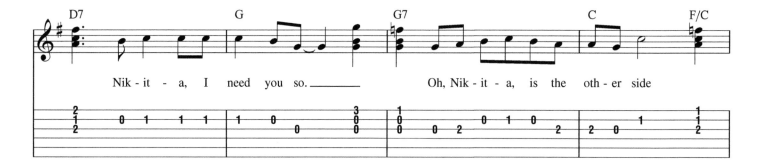

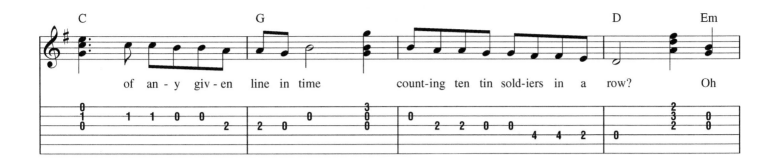

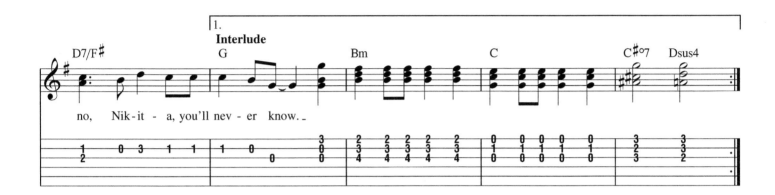

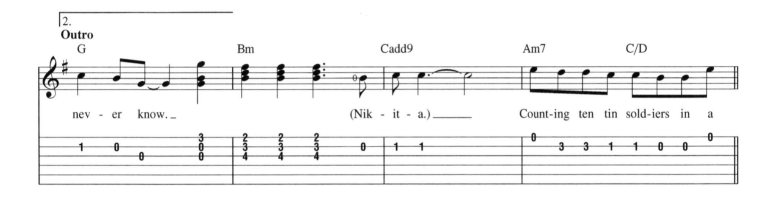

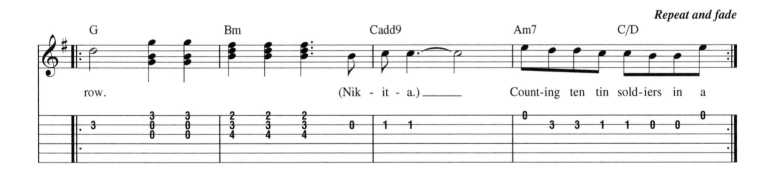

Additional Lyrics

2. Do you ever dream of me?
   Do you ever see the letters that I write?
   When you look up through the wire,
   Nikita, do you count the stars at night?
   And if there comes a time
   Guns and gates no longer hold you in,
   And if you're free to make a choice,
   Just look towards the west and find a friend.

Sacrifice

Words and Music by Elton John and Bernie Taupin

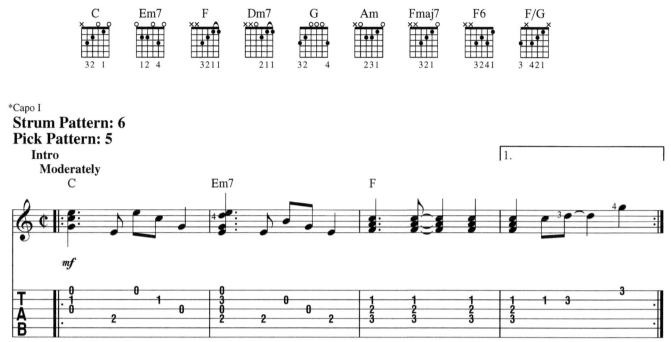

*Capo I

Strum Pattern: 6
Pick Pattern: 5

Intro
Moderately

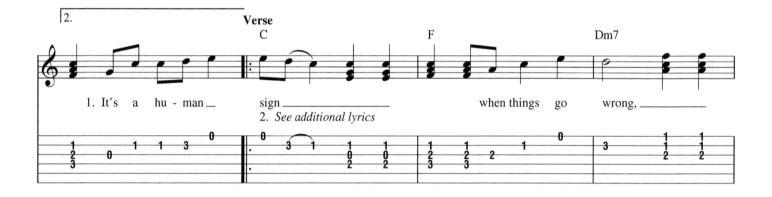

*Optional: To match recording, place capo at 1st fret.

Verse

1. It's a hu-man sign when things go wrong,
2. *See additional lyrics*

when the scent of her lin - gers and temp - ta - tion's strong. In - to the boun-

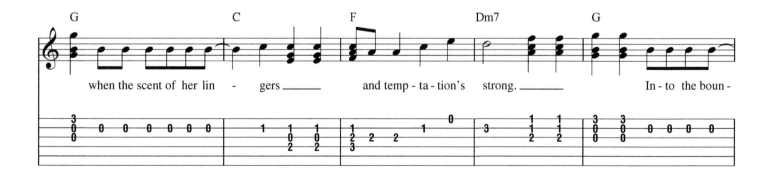

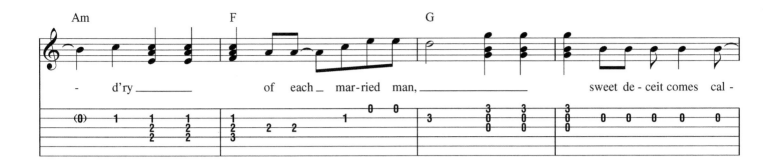

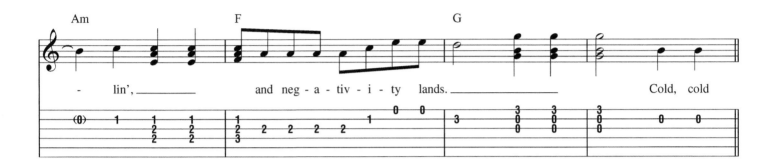

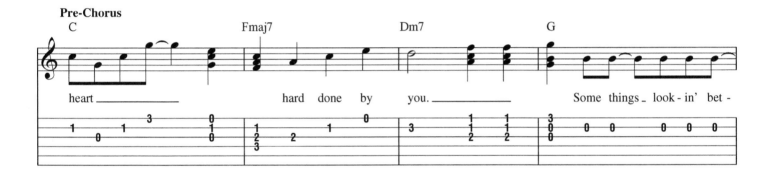

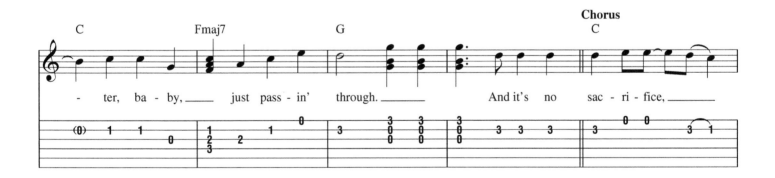

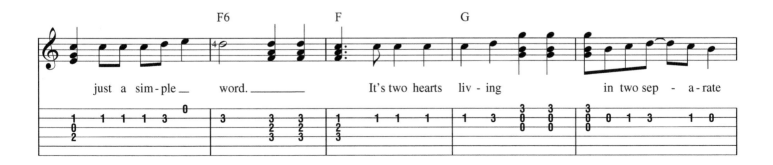

worlds. _____ But it's no sac-ri-fice, _____ no sac-ri-fice, _____

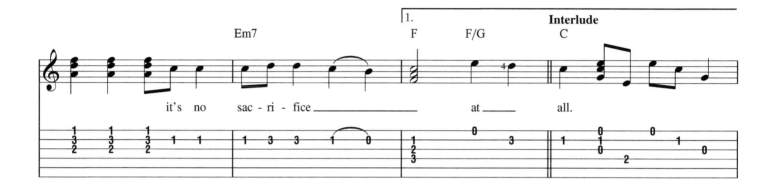

Interlude

it's no sac-ri-fice _____ at _____ all.

_____ at _____

Repeat and fade

Outro

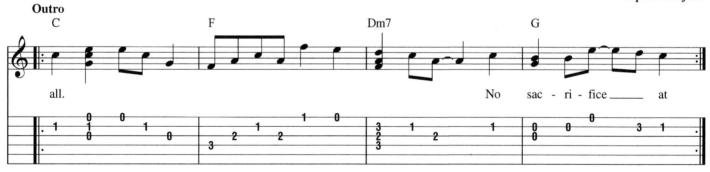

all. No sac-ri-fice _____ at

Additional Lyrics

2. Mutual misunderstanding after the fact,
   Sensitivity builds a prison in the final act.
   We lose direction, no stone unturned,
   No tears to damn you when jealousy burns.

The One

Words and Music by Elton John and Bernie Taupin

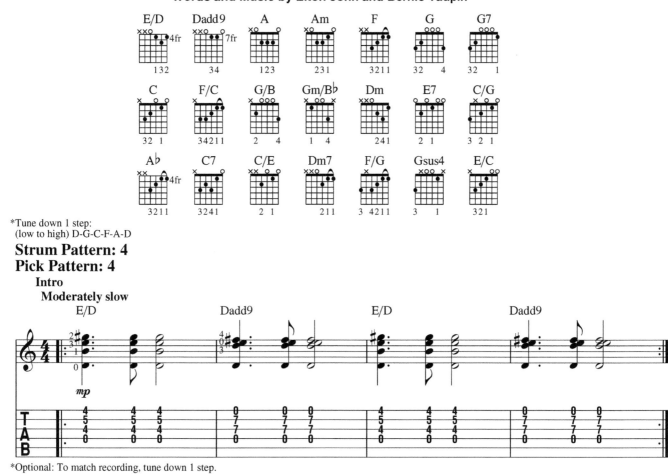

*Tune down 1 step:
(low to high) D-G-C-F-A-D

Strum Pattern: 4
Pick Pattern: 4

Intro
Moderately slow

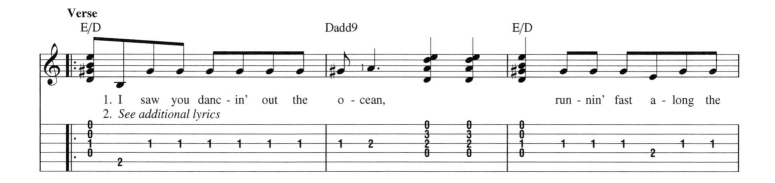

*Optional: To match recording, tune down 1 step.

Verse

1. I saw you danc-in' out the o-cean, run-nin' fast a-long the sand.
2. *See additional lyrics*

A spi-rit born of earth and wa-ter, fire fly-in' from your

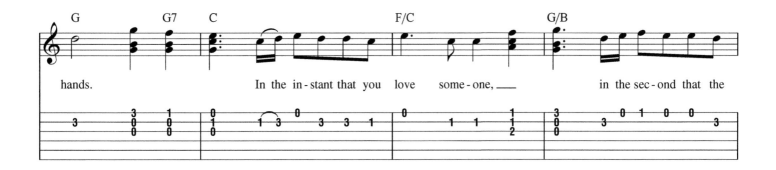

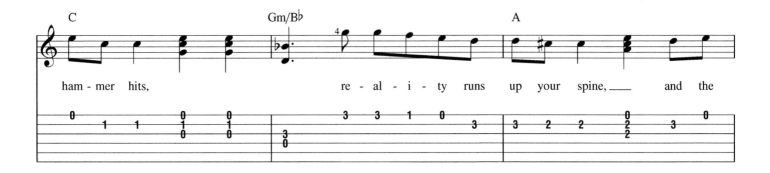

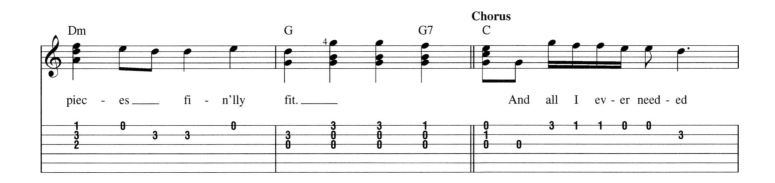

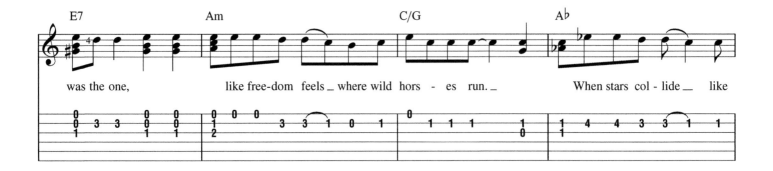

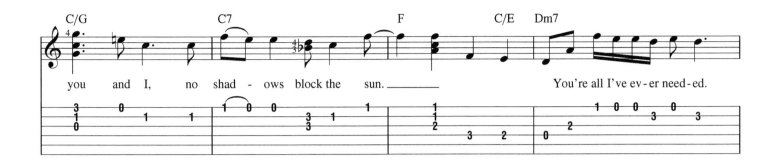

you and I, no shad - ows block the sun. _____ You're all I've ev - er need - ed.

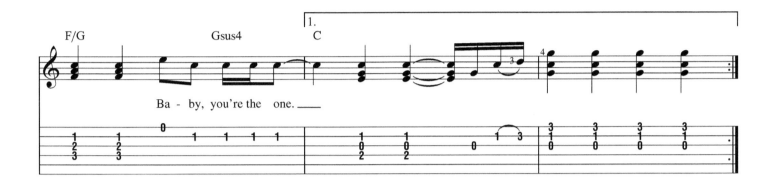

Ba - by, you're the one. _____

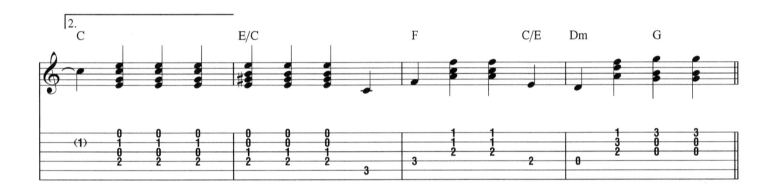

Repeat and fade

Outro

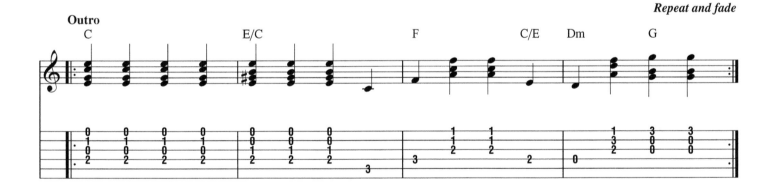

Additional Lyrics

2. There are caravans we follow,
   Drunken nights in dark hotels,
   When chances breathe between the silence,
   Where sex and love no longer gel.
   For each man in his time is Cain,
   Until he walks along the beach
   And sees his future in the water,
   A long-lost heart within his reach.

Can You Feel the Love Tonight

from Walt Disney Pictures' THE LION KING

Music by Elton John
Lyrics by Tim Rice

*Tune down 1 step:
(low to high) D-G-C-F-A-D

Strum Pattern: 4
Pick Pattern: 4

Verse
Ballad

1. There's a calm __ sur - ren - der to the rush __ of

*Optional: To match recording, tune down 1 step.

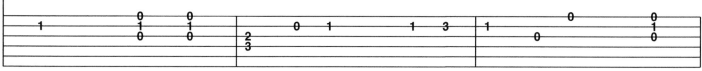

day, when the heat __ of the roll - ing world __

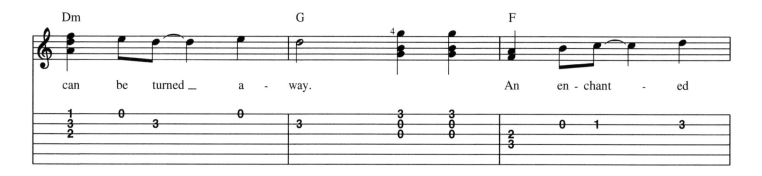

can be turned __ a - way. An en - chant - ed

mo - ment, and it sees __ me through.

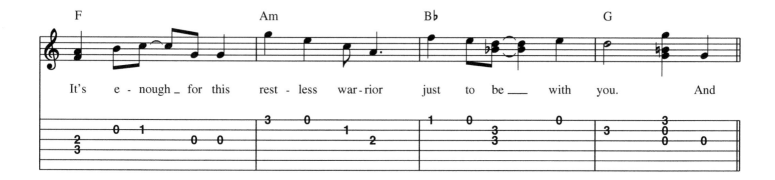

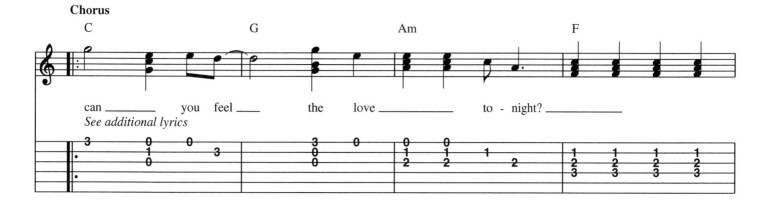

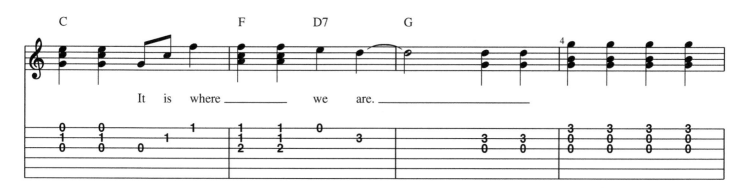

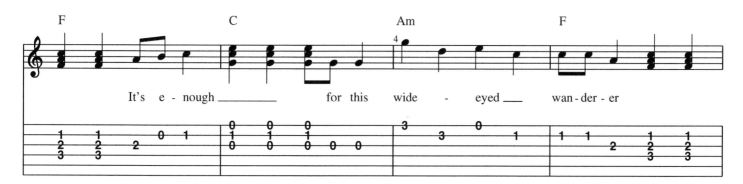

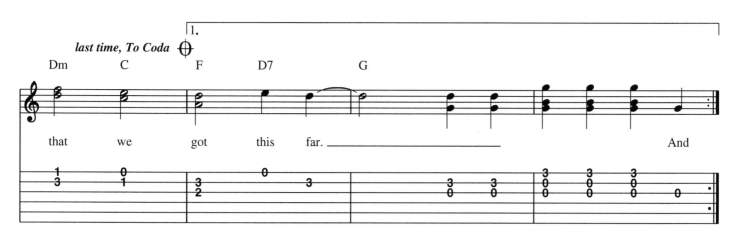

2.

ver - y best.

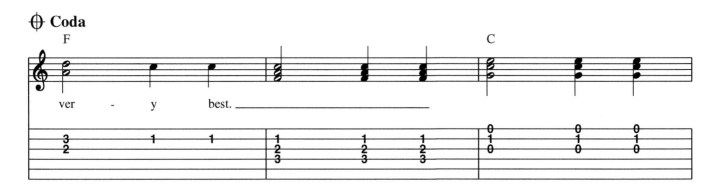

🎯 **Coda**

ver - y best.

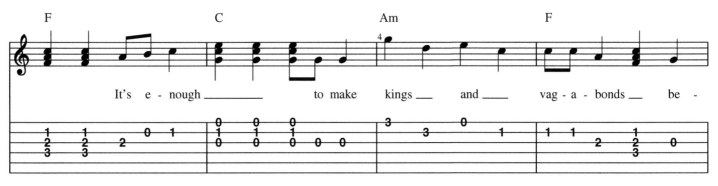

It's e - nough _____ to make kings _____ and _____ vag - a - bonds _____ be -

lieve the ver - y best. _____

Additional Lyrics

2. There's a time for ev'ryone,
   If they only learn
   That the twisting kaleidoscope
   Moves us all in turn.
   There's a rhyme and reason
   To the wild outdoors
   When the heart of this star-crossed voyager
   Beats in time with yours.

Chorus And can you feel the love tonight,
   How it's laid to rest?
   It's enough to make kings and vagabonds
   Believe the very best.

Believe

Words and Music by Elton John and Bernie Taupin

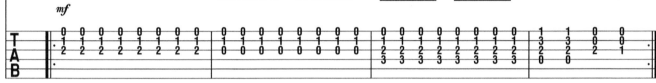

*Tune down 1 step:
(low to high) D-G-C-F-A-D

Strum Pattern: 3, 4
Pick Pattern: 5

Intro
Slow Rock

*Optional: To match recording, tune down 1 step.

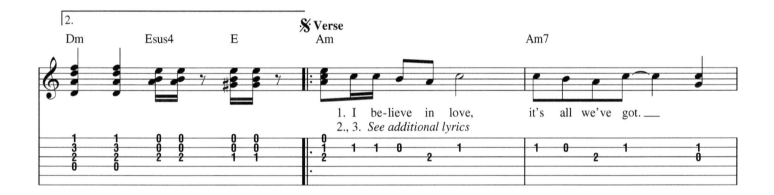

1. I be-lieve in love, it's all we've got. ___
2., 3. *See additional lyrics*

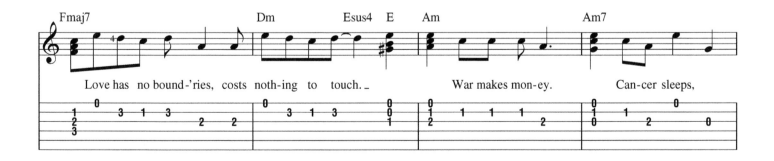

Love has no bound-'ries, costs noth-ing to touch. ___ War makes mon-ey. Can-cer sleeps,

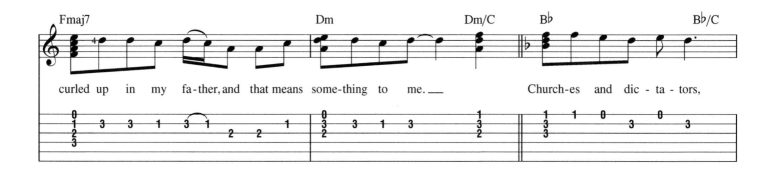

curled up in my fa-ther, and that means some-thing to me.___ Church-es and dic - ta - tors,

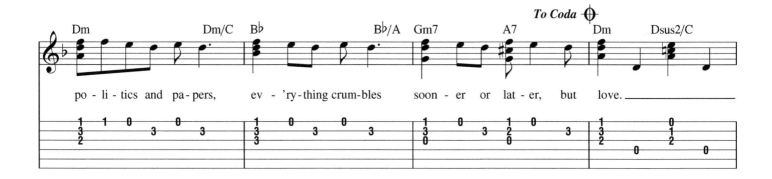

po - li - tics and pa - pers, ev - 'ry-thing crum-bles soon - er or lat - er, but love.___

___ I be-lieve___ in love.___

Interlude

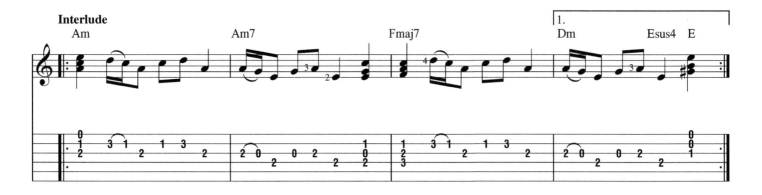

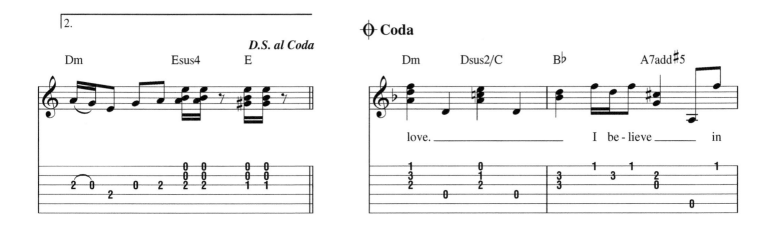

Additional Lyrics

2. I believe in love, it's all we've got,
   Love has no bound'ries, no borders to cross.
   Love is simple. Hate breeds
   Those who think difference is the child of disease.
   Father and son make love and guns.
   Families together kill someone
   Without love.
   I believe in love.

3. Without love, I wouldn't believe
   In anything that lives and breathes.
   Without love, I'd have no anger.
   I wouldn't believe in the right to stand here.
   Without love, I wouldn't believe.
   I couldn't believe in you, and I
   Wouldn't believe in me
   Without love.
   I believe in love.
   I believe in love.
   I believe in love.

Circle of Life

from Walt Disney Pictures' THE LION KING

Music by Elton John
Lyrics by Tim Rice

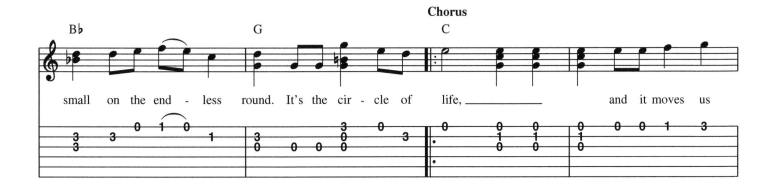

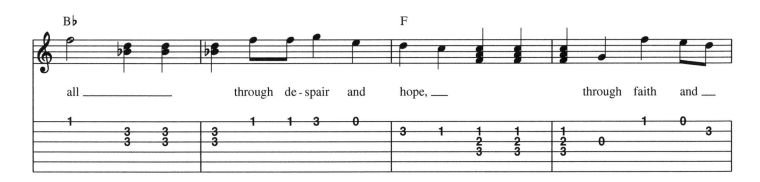

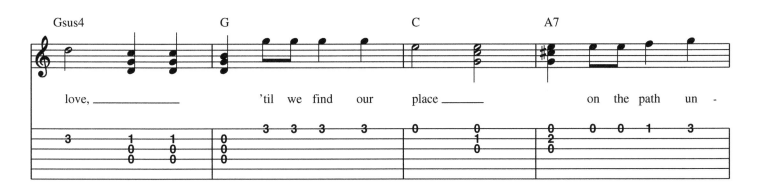

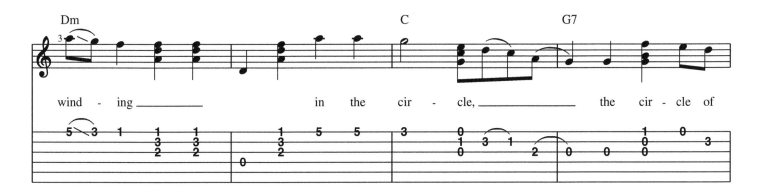

Blessed

Words and Music by Elton John and Bernie Taupin

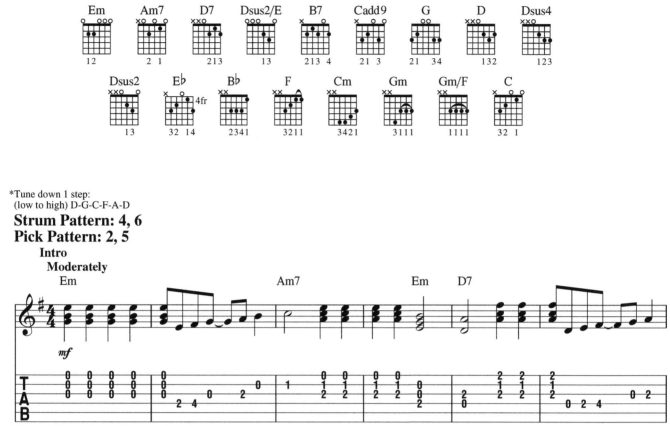

*Tune down 1 step:
(low to high) D-G-C-F-A-D

Strum Pattern: 4, 6
Pick Pattern: 2, 5

Intro
Moderately

*Optional: To match recording, tune down 1 step.

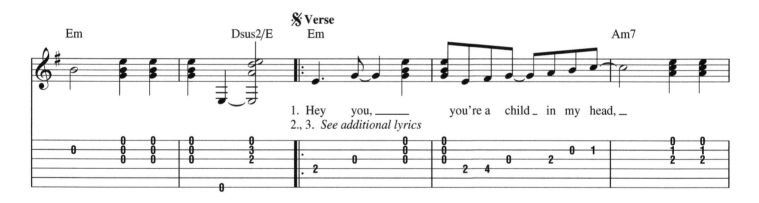

Verse

1. Hey you, _____ you're a child _ in my head, _

2., 3. *See additional lyrics*

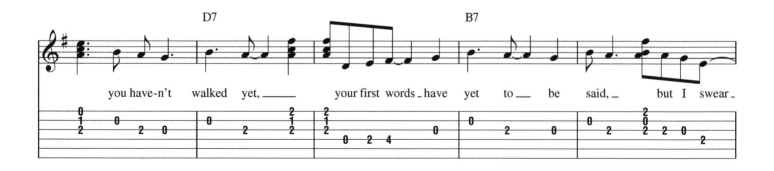

you have-n't walked yet, _____ your first words _ have yet to be said, _ but I swear

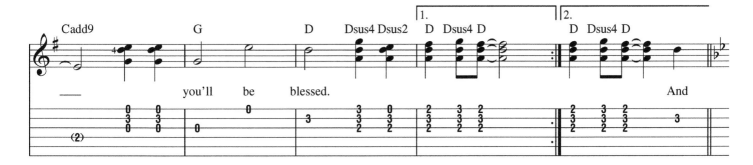

youʼll be blessed. And

Chorus

you, _____ youʼll be blessed, _ youʼll have the best, _ I pro-mise you that. _ Iʼll pick a star from the sky, _

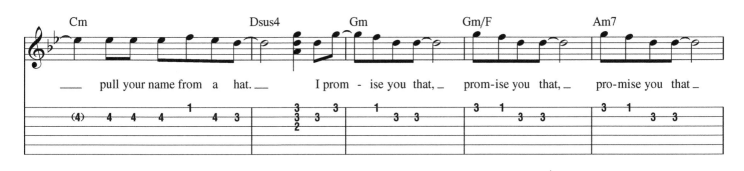

_____ pull your name from a hat. _ I prom - ise you that, _ prom-ise you that, _ pro-mise you that _

To Coda

D.S. al Coda
(take 2nd ending)

youʼll _____ be _____ blessed. _

Outro

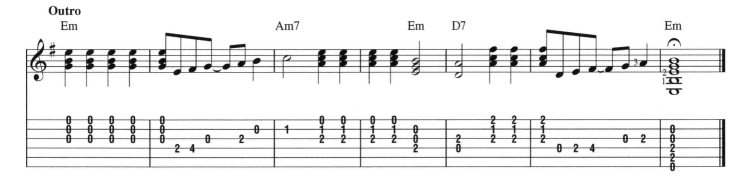

Additional Lyrics

2. I know youʼre still just a dream,
   Your eyes might be green,
   Or the bluest that Iʼve ever seen.
   Anyway, youʼll be blessed.

3. I need you, before Iʼm too old,
   To have and to hold,
   To walk with you and watch you grow,
   And know that youʼre blessed.

Something About the Way You Look Tonight

Words and Music by Elton John and Bernie Taupin

*Tune down 1/2 step:
(low to high) Eb-Ab-Db-Gb-Bb-Eb

Strum Pattern: 2, 4
Pick Pattern: 4, 5

*Optional: To match recording, tune down 1/2 step.

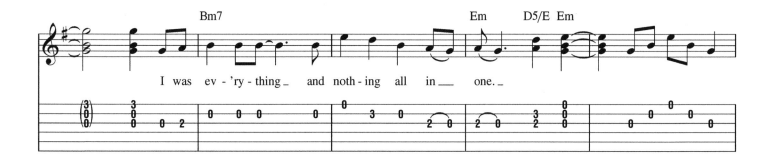

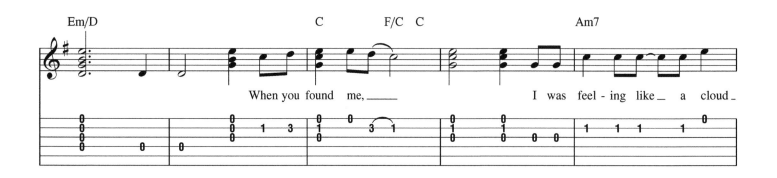

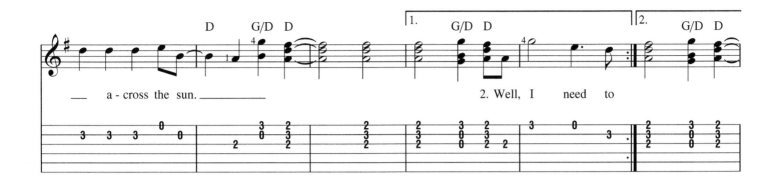

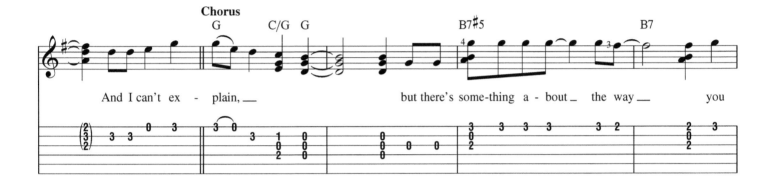

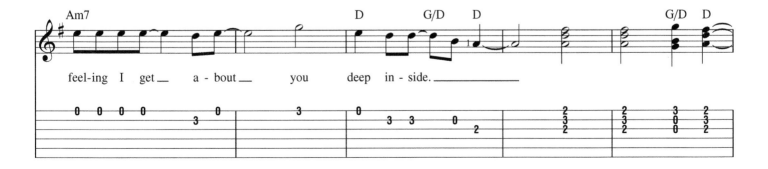

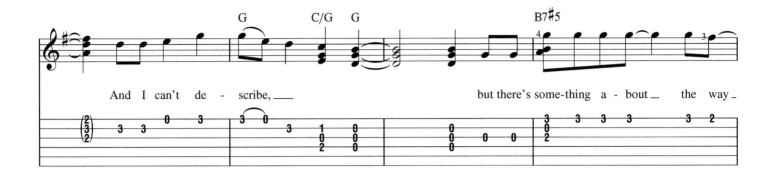

And I can't de - scribe, _____ but there's some-thing a - bout_ the way_

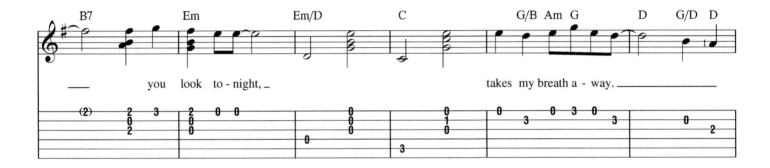

___ you look to - night, _ takes my breath a - way. _____

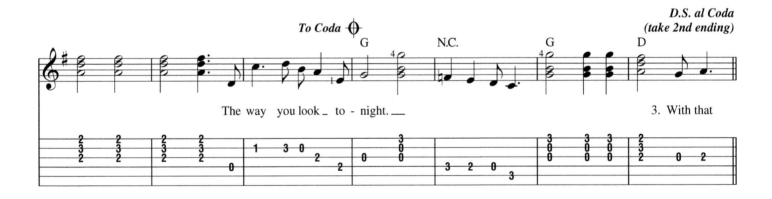

To Coda ⊕

D.S. al Coda
(take 2nd ending)

The way you look _ to - night. _ 3. With that

⊕ **Coda**

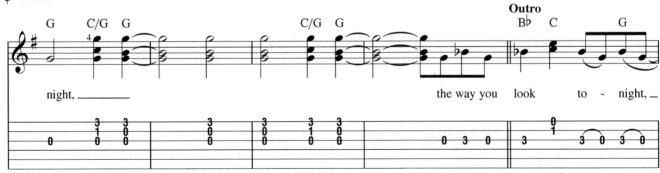

Outro

night, _____ the way you look to - night, _

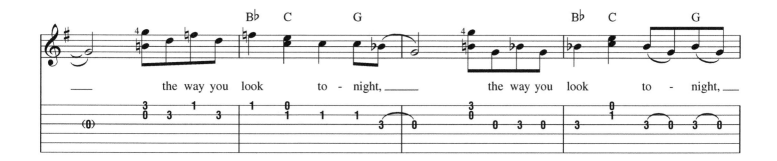

the way you look to - night, _____ the way you look to - night, __

_____ the way you look to - night, _____ the way you look

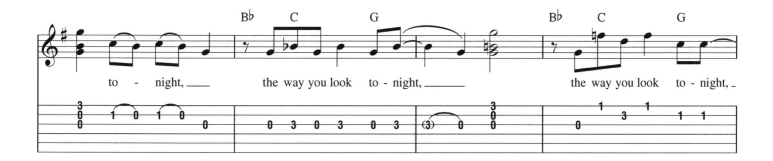

to - night, __ the way you look to - night, _____ the way you look to - night, _

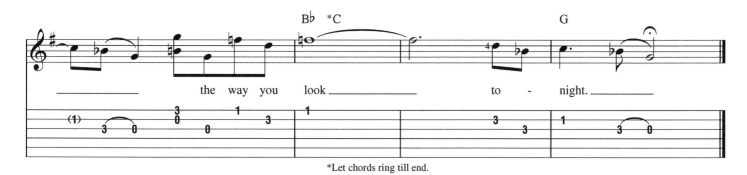

_____ the way you look _____ to - night. _____

*Let chords ring till end.

Additional Lyrics

2. Well, I need to tell you
   How you light up ev'ry second of the day,
   But in the moonlight,
   You just shine like a beacon of the bay.

3. With that smile,
   You pull the deepest secrets from my heart.
   In all honesty,
   I'm speechless and I don't know where to start.

Written in the Stars

from Elton John and Tim Rice's AIDA

Music by Elton John
Lyrics by Tim Rice

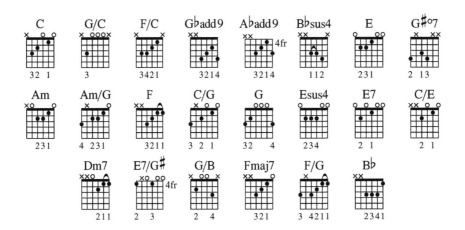

Strum Pattern: 4
Pick Pattern: 1

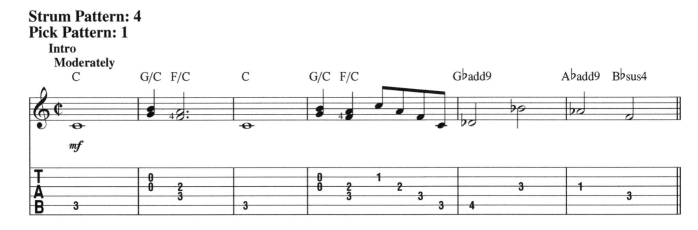

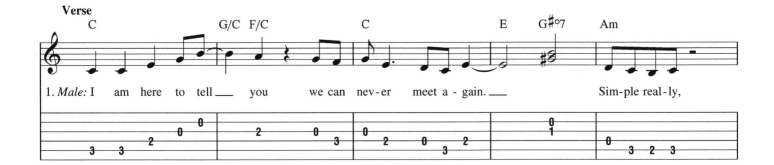

1. *Male:* I am here to tell ___ you we can nev-er meet a - gain. ___ Sim-ple real-ly,

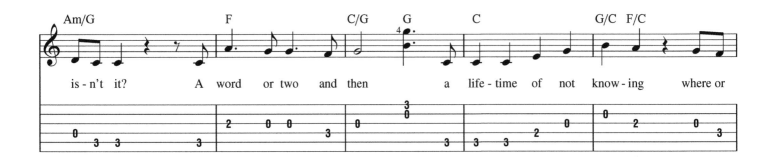

is - n't it? A word or two and then a life - time of not know - ing where or

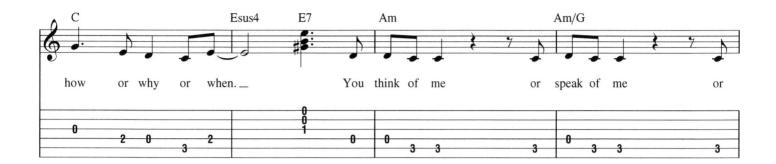

how or why or when. ___ You think of me or speak of me or

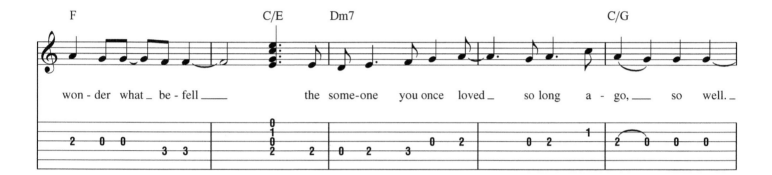

won - der what _ be - fell ____ the some-one you once loved _ so long a - go, ___ so well. _

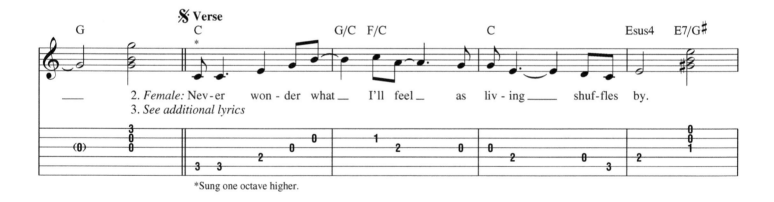

2. *Female:* Nev - er won - der what _ I'll feel _ as liv - ing ____ shuf-fles by.
3. *See additional lyrics*

*Sung one octave higher.

You don't have to ask me, and I need not re - ply. ____ Ev-'ry mo - ment of _

_____ my life _____ from now un - til I die _____ I will think or

dream of you and fail _____ to un - der - stand how a per - fect love _____ can

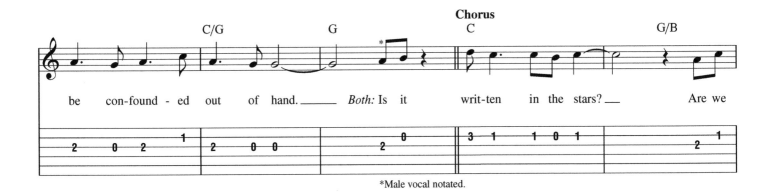

Chorus

be con-found - ed out of hand. _____ *Both:* Is it writ-ten in the stars? _____ Are we

*Male vocal notated.

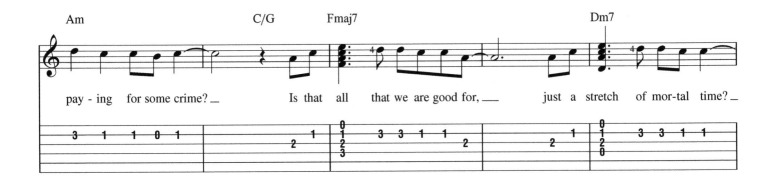

pay - ing for some crime? _ Is that all that we are good for, _____ just a stretch of mor-tal time? _

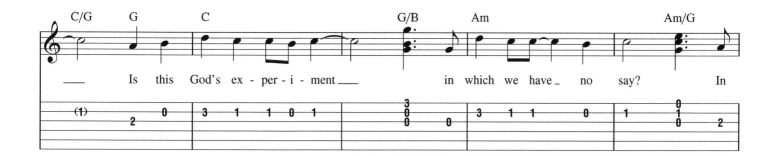

Is this God's ex-per-i-ment ____ in which we have __ no say? In

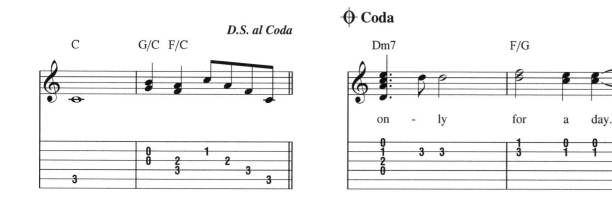

To Coda ⊕

Interlude

which we're giv-en par-a-dise, but on — ly for a day. ____

D.S. al Coda

⊕ **Coda**

Outro

on — ly for a day. _____

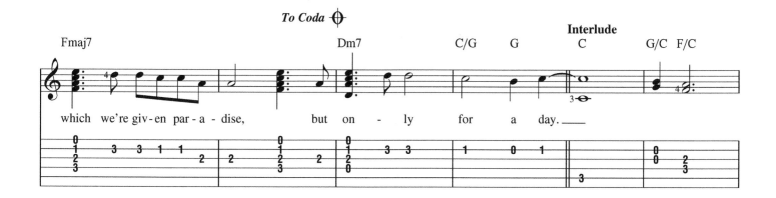

rit.

Additional Lyrics

3. *Male:* Nothing can be altered. Oh, there is nothing to decide,
   No escape, no change of heart, nor any place to hide.
Female: You are all I'll ever want, but this I am denied.
   Sometimes in my darkest thoughts I wish I never learned
Both: What it is to be in love and have that love returned.

I Want Love

Words and Music by Elton John and Bernie Taupin

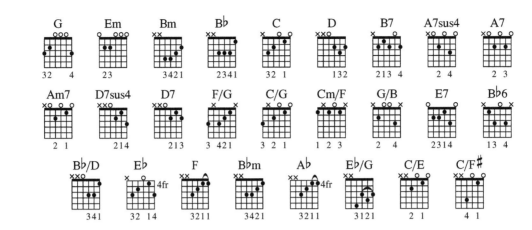

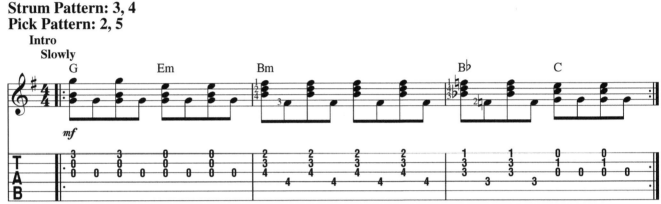

*Capo II

Strum Pattern: 3, 4
Pick Pattern: 2, 5

Intro
Slowly

*Optional: To match recording, place capo at 2nd fret.

Verse

1. I want love, ___ but it's im-pos-si-ble. ___ A man like me ___ so ir-re-spon-si-ble. ___ A man like me is dead in plac-es oth-er men ___ feel

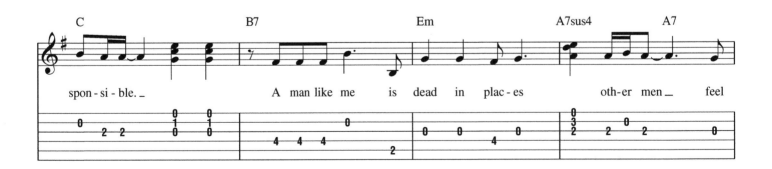

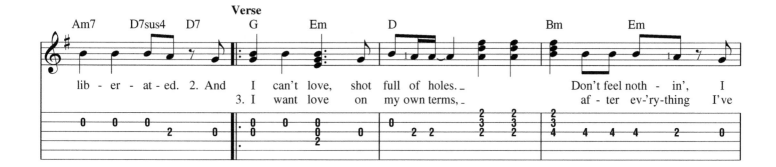

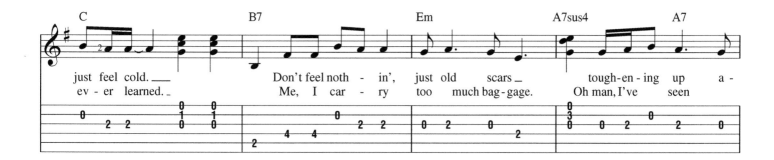

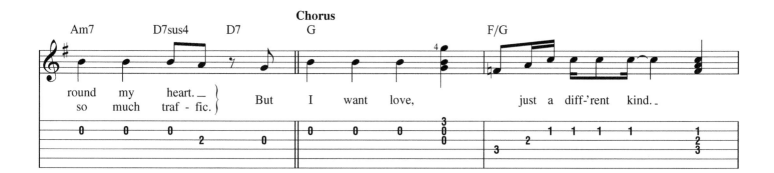

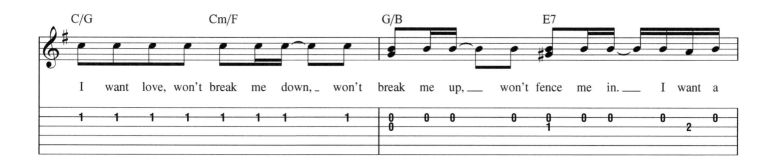

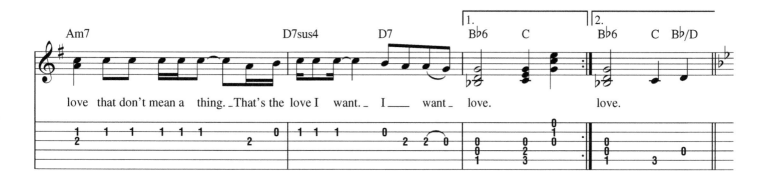

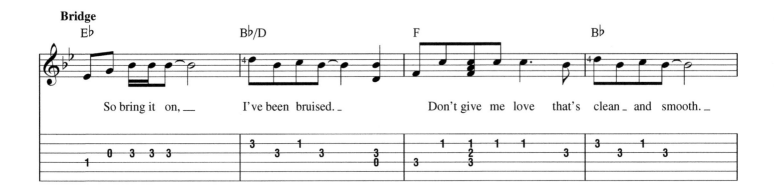

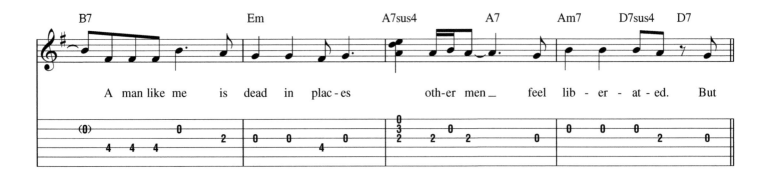

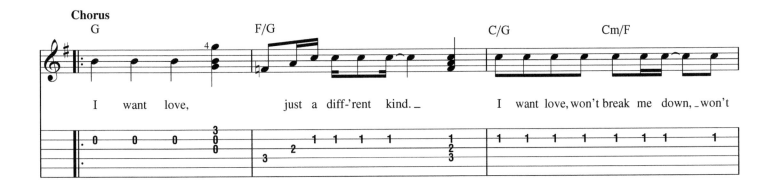

Chorus

I want love, just a diff-'rent kind. I want love, won't break me down, won't

break me up, won't fence me in. I want a love that don't mean a thing. That's the

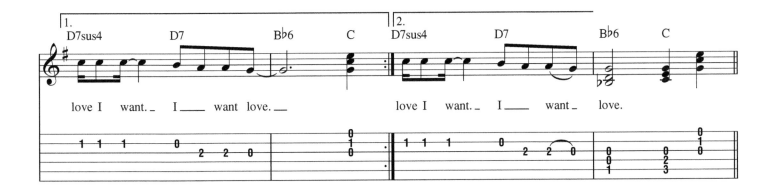

1. love I want. I want love.

2. love I want. I want love.

Outro

This Train Don't Stop There Anymore

Words and Music by Elton John and Bernie Taupin

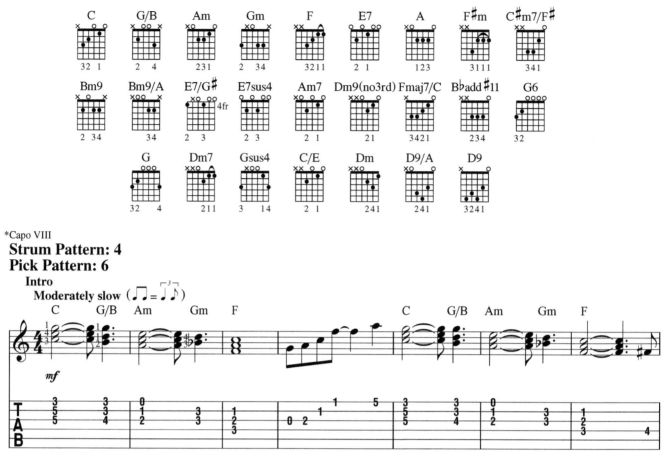

*Capo VIII

Strum Pattern: 4
Pick Pattern: 6

Intro
Moderately slow

*Optional: To match recording, place capo at 8th fret.

Verse

1. You may not be-lieve it, but I don't be-lieve in mi-ra-cles an-y-more.
2. *See additional lyrics*

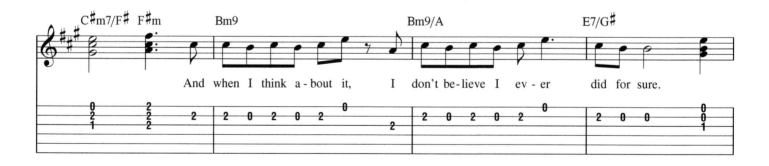

And when I think a-bout it, I don't be-lieve I ev-er did for sure.

All the things I've said in songs, __ all the pur - ple prose you've bought from me: __

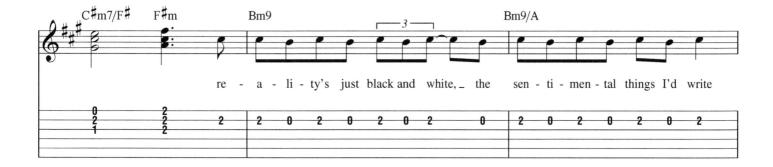

re - a - li - ty's just black and white, _ the sen - ti - men - tal things I'd write

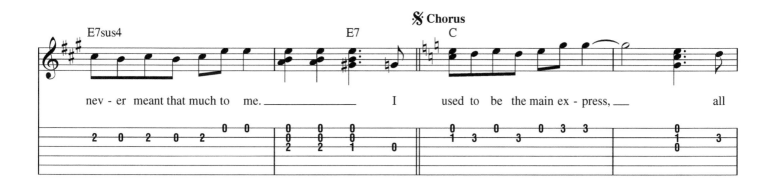

nev - er meant that much to me. _____ I used to be the main ex - press, __ all

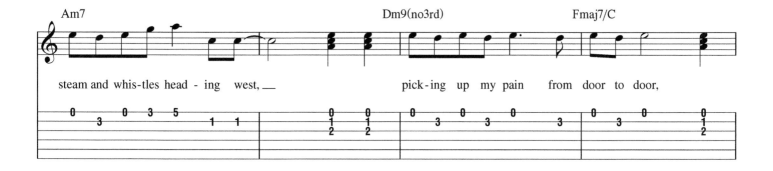

steam and whis - tles head - ing west, __ pick - ing up my pain from door to door,

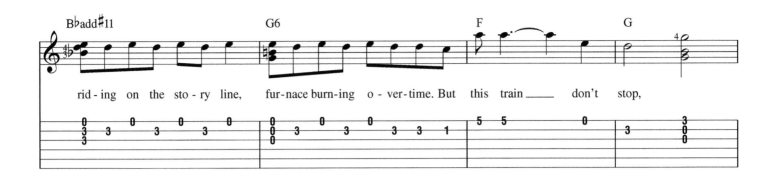

ri - ding on the sto - ry line, fur-nace burn-ing o - ver-time. But this train ___ don't stop,

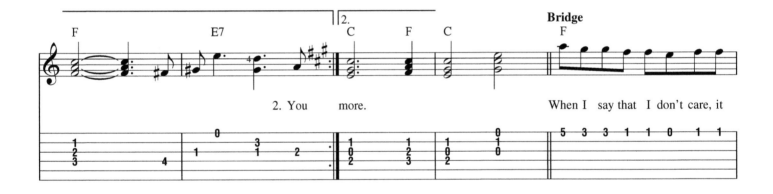

this train ___ don't stop, this train ___ don't stop there ___ an - y - more. ___

2. You more.

Bridge

When I say that I don't care, it

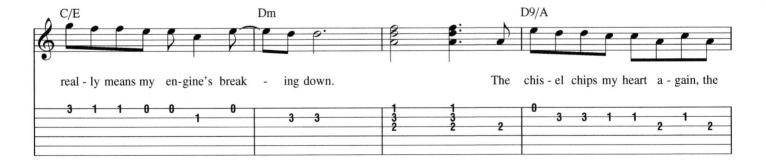

real - ly means my en-gine's break - ing down. The chis - el chips my heart a - gain, the

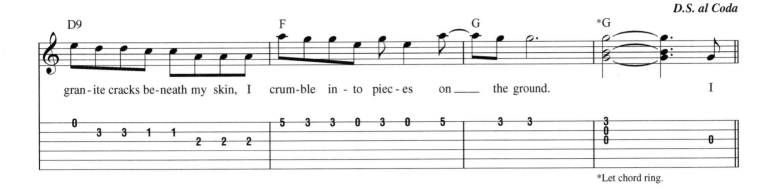

gran-ite cracks be-neath my skin, I crum-ble in-to piec-es on ___ the ground.   I

Let chord ring.

⊕ Coda

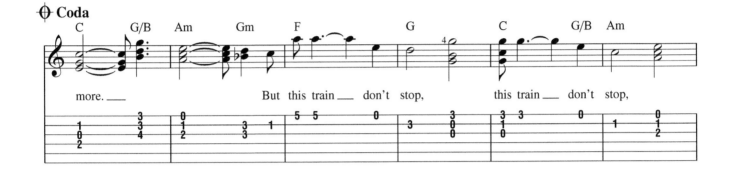

more. ___   But this train ___ don't stop,   this train ___ don't stop,

Outro

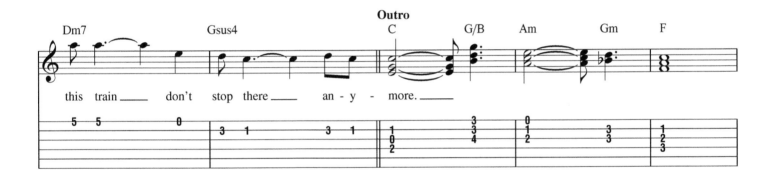

this train ___ don't stop there ___ an-y-more. ___

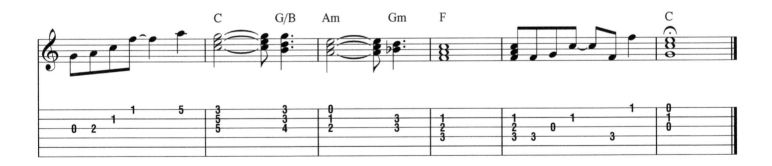

Additional Lyrics

2. You don't need to hear it,
   But I'm dried up and sick to death of love.
   And if you need to know it,
   I never really understood that stuff.
   All the stars and bleeding hearts,
   All the tears that welled up in my eyes
   Never meant a thing to me.
   Read 'em, as they say, and weep!
   I've never felt enough to cry.

EASY GUITAR
WITH NOTES & TAB

This series features simplified arrangements with notes, tab, chord charts, and strum and pick patterns.

MIXED FOLIOS

00702287	Acoustic	$19.99
00702002	Acoustic Rock Hits for Easy Guitar	$15.99
00702166	All-Time Best Guitar Collection	$19.99
00702232	Best Acoustic Songs for Easy Guitar	$16.99
00119835	Best Children's Songs	$16.99
00703055	The Big Book of Nursery Rhymes & Children's Songs	$16.99
00698978	Big Christmas Collection	$19.99
00702394	Bluegrass Songs for Easy Guitar	$15.99
00289632	Bohemian Rhapsody	$19.99
00703387	Celtic Classics	$16.99
00224808	Chart Hits of 2016-2017	$14.99
00267383	Chart Hits of 2017-2018	$14.99
00334293	Chart Hits of 2019-2020	$16.99
00403479	Chart Hits of 2021-2022	$16.99
00702149	Children's Christian Songbook	$9.99
00702028	Christmas Classics	$8.99
00101779	Christmas Guitar	$14.99
00702141	Classic Rock	$8.95
00159642	Classical Melodies	$12.99
00253933	Disney/Pixar's Coco	$16.99
00702203	CMT's 100 Greatest Country Songs	$34.99
00702283	The Contemporary Christian Collection	$16.99

00196954	Contemporary Disney	$19.99
00702239	Country Classics for Easy Guitar	$24.99
00702257	Easy Acoustic Guitar Songs	$17.99
00702041	Favorite Hymns for Easy Guitar	$12.99
00222701	Folk Pop Songs	$17.99
00126894	Frozen	$14.99
00333922	Frozen 2	$14.99
00702286	Glee	$16.99
00702160	The Great American Country Songbook	$19.99
00702148	Great American Gospel for Guitar	$14.99
00702050	Great Classical Themes for Easy Guitar	$9.99
00275088	The Greatest Showman	$17.99
00148030	Halloween Guitar Songs	$14.99
00702273	Irish Songs	$14.99
00192503	Jazz Classics for Easy Guitar	$16.99
00702275	Jazz Favorites for Easy Guitar	$17.99
00702274	Jazz Standards for Easy Guitar	$19.99
00702162	Jumbo Easy Guitar Songbook	$24.99
00232285	La La Land	$16.99
00702258	Legends of Rock	$14.99
00702189	MTV's 100 Greatest Pop Songs	$34.99
00702272	1950s Rock	$16.99
00702271	1960s Rock	$16.99
00702270	1970s Rock	$24.99
00702269	1980s Rock	$16.99

00702268	1990s Rock	$24.99
00369043	Rock Songs for Kids	$14.99
00109725	Once	$14.99
00702187	Selections from O Brother Where Art Thou?	$19.99
00702178	100 Songs for Kids	$16.99
00702515	Pirates of the Caribbean	$17.99
00702125	Praise and Worship for Guitar	$14.99
00287930	Songs from *A Star Is Born, The Greatest Showman, La La Land,* and More Movie Musicals	$16.99
00702285	Southern Rock Hits	$12.99
00156420	Star Wars Music	$16.99
00121535	30 Easy Celtic Guitar Solos	$16.99
00244654	Top Hits of 2017	$14.99
00283786	Top Hits of 2018	$14.99
00302269	Top Hits of 2019	$14.99
00355779	Top Hits of 2020	$14.99
00374083	Top Hits of 2021	$16.99
00702294	Top Worship Hits	$17.99
00702255	VH1's 100 Greatest Hard Rock Songs	$34.99
00702175	VH1's 100 Greatest Songs of Rock and Roll	$34.99
00702253	Wicked	$12.99

ARTIST COLLECTIONS

00702267	AC/DC for Easy Guitar	$16.99
00156221	Adele – 25	$16.99
00396889	Adele – 30	$19.99
00702040	Best of the Allman Brothers	$16.99
00702865	J.S. Bach for Easy Guitar	$15.99
00702169	Best of The Beach Boys	$16.99
00702292	The Beatles — 1	$22.99
00125796	Best of Chuck Berry	$16.99
00702201	The Essential Black Sabbath	$15.99
00702250	blink-182 — Greatest Hits	$17.99
02501615	Zac Brown Band — The Foundation	$17.99
02501621	Zac Brown Band — You Get What You Give	$16.99
00702043	Best of Johnny Cash	$17.99
00702090	Eric Clapton's Best	$16.99
00702086	Eric Clapton — from the Album Unplugged	$17.99
00702202	The Essential Eric Clapton	$17.99
00702053	Best of Patsy Cline	$17.99
00222697	Very Best of Coldplay – 2nd Edition	$17.99
00702229	The Very Best of Creedence Clearwater Revival	$16.99
00702145	Best of Jim Croce	$16.99
00702278	Crosby, Stills & Nash	$12.99
14042809	Bob Dylan	$15.99
00702276	Fleetwood Mac — Easy Guitar Collection	$17.99
00139462	The Very Best of Grateful Dead	$16.99
00702136	Best of Merle Haggard	$16.99
00702227	Jimi Hendrix — Smash Hits	$19.99
00702288	Best of Hillsong United	$12.99
00702236	Best of Antonio Carlos Jobim	$15.99

00702245	Elton John — Greatest Hits 1970–2002	$19.99
00129855	Jack Johnson	$17.99
00702204	Robert Johnson	$16.99
00702234	Selections from Toby Keith — 35 Biggest Hits	$12.95
00702003	Kiss	$16.99
00702216	Lynyrd Skynyrd	$17.99
00702182	The Essential Bob Marley	$16.99
00146081	Maroon 5	$14.99
00121925	Bruno Mars – Unorthodox Jukebox	$12.99
00702248	Paul McCartney — All the Best	$14.99
00125484	The Best of MercyMe	$12.99
00702209	Steve Miller Band — Young Hearts (Greatest Hits)	$12.95
00124167	Jason Mraz	$15.99
00702096	Best of Nirvana	$16.99
00702211	The Offspring — Greatest Hits	$17.99
00138026	One Direction	$17.99
00702030	Best of Roy Orbison	$17.99
00702144	Best of Ozzy Osbourne	$14.99
00702279	Tom Petty	$17.99
00102911	Pink Floyd	$17.99
00702139	Elvis Country Favorites	$19.99
00702293	The Very Best of Prince	$19.99
00699415	Best of Queen for Guitar	$16.99
00109279	Best of R.E.M.	$14.99
00702208	Red Hot Chili Peppers — Greatest Hits	$17.99
00198960	The Rolling Stones	$17.99
00174793	The Very Best of Santana	$16.99
00702196	Best of Bob Seger	$16.99
00146046	Ed Sheeran	$17.99

00702252	Frank Sinatra — Nothing But the Best	$12.99
00702010	Best of Rod Stewart	$17.99
00702049	Best of George Strait	$17.99
00702259	Taylor Swift for Easy Guitar	$15.99
00359800	Taylor Swift – Easy Guitar Anthology	$24.99
00702260	Taylor Swift — Fearless	$14.99
00139727	Taylor Swift — 1989	$19.99
00115960	Taylor Swift — Red	$16.99
00253667	Taylor Swift — Reputation	$17.99
00702290	Taylor Swift — Speak Now	$16.99
00232849	Chris Tomlin Collection – 2nd Edition	$14.99
00702226	Chris Tomlin — See the Morning	$12.95
00148643	Train	$14.99
00702427	U2 — 18 Singles	$19.99
00702108	Best of Stevie Ray Vaughan	$17.99
00279005	The Who	$14.99
00702123	Best of Hank Williams	$15.99
00194548	Best of John Williams	$14.99
00702228	Neil Young — Greatest Hits	$17.99
00119133	Neil Young — Harvest	$14.99

Visit Hal Leonard online at **halleonard.com**

HAL•LEONARD GUITAR PLAY-ALONG

Complete song lists available online.

This series will help you play your favorite songs quickly and easily. Just follow **INCLUDES TAB** the tab and listen to the audio to the hear how the guitar should sound, and then play along using the separate backing tracks. Audio files also include software to slow down the tempo without changing pitch. The melody and lyrics are included in the book so that you can sing or simply follow along.

Prices, contents, and availability subject to change without notice.

HAL•LEONARD®
www.halleonard.com

Get Better at Guitar

...with these Great Guitar Instruction Books from Hal Leonard!

101 GUITAR TIPS
STUFF ALL THE PROS KNOW AND USE
by Adam St. James
This book contains invaluable guidance on everything from scales and music theory to truss rod adjustments, proper recording studio set-ups, and much more.
00695737 Book/Online Audio $17.99

AMAZING PHRASING
by Tom Kolb
This book/audio pack explores all the main components necessary for crafting well-balanced rhythmic and melodic phrases. It also explains how these phrases are put together to form cohesive solos. The companion audio contains 89 demo tracks, most with full-band backing.
00695583 Book/Online Audio $22.99

ARPEGGIOS FOR THE MODERN GUITARIST
by Tom Kolb
Using this no-nonsense book with online audio, guitarists will learn to apply and execute all types of arpeggio forms using a variety of techniques, including alternate picking, sweep picking, tapping, string skipping, and legato.
00695862 Book/Online Audio $22.99

BLUES YOU CAN USE
by John Ganapes
This comprehensive source for learning blues guitar is designed to develop both your lead and rhythm playing. Includes: 21 complete solos • blues chords, progressions and riffs • turnarounds • movable scales and soloing techniques • string bending • utilizing the entire fingerboard • and more.
00142420 Book/Online Media $22.99

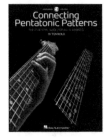

CONNECTING PENTATONIC PATTERNS
by Tom Kolb
If you've been finding yourself trapped in the pentatonic box, this book is for you! This hands-on book with online audio offers examples for guitar players of all levels, from beginner to advanced. Study this book faithfully, and soon you'll be soloing all over the neck with the greatest of ease.
00696445 Book/Online Audio $24.99

FRETBOARD MASTERY
by Troy Stetina
Untangle the mysterious regions of the guitar fretboard and unlock your potential. This book familiarizes you with all the shapes you need to know by applying them in real musical examples, thereby reinforcing and reaffirming your newfound knowledge.
00695331 Book/Online Audio $22.99

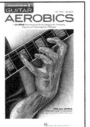

GUITAR AEROBICS
by Troy Nelson
Here is a daily dose of guitar "vitamins" to keep your chops fine tuned! Musical styles include rock, blues, jazz, metal, country, and funk. Techniques taught include alternate picking, arpeggios, sweep picking, string skipping, legato, string bending, and rhythm guitar.
00695946 Book/Online Audio $24.99

GUITAR CLUES
OPERATION PENTATONIC
by Greg Koch
Whether you're new to improvising or have been doing it for a while, this book/audio pack will provide loads of delicious licks and tricks that you can use right away, from volume swells and chicken pickin' to intervallic and chordal ideas.
00695827 Book/Online Audio $19.99

PAT METHENY – GUITAR ETUDES
Over the years, in many master classes and workshops around the world, Pat has demonstrated the kind of daily workout he puts himself through. This book includes a collection of 14 guitar etudes he created to help you limber up, improve picking technique and build finger independence.
00696587 ....$17.99

PICTURE CHORD ENCYCLOPEDIA
This comprehensive guitar chord resource for all playing styles and levels features five voicings of 44 chord qualities for all twelve keys – 2,640 chords in all! For each, there is a clearly illustrated chord frame, as well as *an actual photo* of the chord being played!.
00695224 ....$22.99

RHYTHM GUITAR 365
by Troy Nelson
This book provides 365 exercises – one for every day of the year! – to keep your rhythm chops fine tuned. Topics covered include: chord theory; the fundamentals of rhythm; fingerpicking; strum patterns; diatonic and non-diatonic progressions; triads; major and minor keys; and more.
00103627 Book/Online Audio $27.99

SCALE CHORD RELATIONSHIPS
by Michael Mueller & Jeff Schroedl
This book/audio pack explains how to: recognize keys • analyze chord progressions • use the modes • play over nondiatonic harmony • use harmonic and melodic minor scales • use symmetrical scales • incorporate exotic scales • and much more!
00695563 Book/Online Audio $17.99

SPEED MECHANICS FOR LEAD GUITAR
by Troy Stetina
Take your playing to the stratosphere with this advanced lead book which will help you develop speed and precision in today's explosive playing styles. Learn the fastest ways to achieve speed and control, secrets to make your practice time really count, and how to open your ears and make your musical ideas more solid and tangible.
00699323 Book/Online Audio $22.99

TOTAL ROCK GUITAR
by Troy Stetina
This comprehensive source for learning rock guitar is designed to develop both lead and rhythm playing. It covers: getting a tone that rocks • open chords, power chords and barre chords • riffs, scales and licks • string bending, strumming, and harmonics • and more.
00695246 Book/Online Audio $22.99

Guitar World Presents STEVE VAI'S GUITAR WORKOUT
In this book, Steve Vai reveals his path to virtuoso enlightenment with two challenging guitar workouts – one 10-hour and one 30-hour – which include scale and chord exercises, ear training, sight-reading, music theory, and much more.
00119643 ....$16.99

Order these and more publications from your favorite music retailer at
halleonard.com

0322
032